What *Every* Woman
Needs to Know
On the Trail

By **Kim Lipker**

MENASHA RIDGE PRESS
www.menasharidge.com

Printed on recycled paper

Library of Congress Cataloging-in-Publication Data

Lipker, Kim, 1969–
    Smart & savvy hiking: what every woman needs to know on the trail/
by Kim Lipker. —1st ed.
        p. cm.
    ISBN-13: 978-0-89732-671-1
    ISBN-10: 0-89732-671-7
    1. Hiking for women—Guidebooks. I. Title. II. Title: Smart and savvy
hiking.
    GV199.58.L57 2008
    796.51082—dc22
                                                        2008046168

Cover design by Scott McGrew
Text design by Travis Bryant and Annie Long
Cover photograph © BlueMoon Stock/Alamy
Interior photographs: Pages xvi and 1, Tom Wald; page 27, Arnau Design;
    pages 28–29, Gas PR; pages 78–79, Claudia D's Portfolio; pages 92–
    93, Arpad Benedek; page 131, Kaspar Photo Art; pages 138–139,
    Anthony Brown Photography; pages 156–157, Gaby Jalbert; page
    187, Saturated Photography; pages 188–189, Mad Hadders Photo;
    pages 212–213, Leading Lights Photography; page 219, Kaspar Photo
    Art; page 222, Alan Lemire Photography
Indexing by Rich Carlson

Menasha Ridge Press
P.O. Box 43673
Birmingham, Alabama 35243
www.menasharidge.com

My grandmother started walking 5 miles a day when she was 60. She's 93 today and we don't know where the hell she is.

—*Ellen DeGeneres*

TRAILHEAD

(Continued on next page)

TRAIL HEAD *(continued)*

Acknowledgments

I cannot thank the following people enough!

Ruth and Roger Lipker, for everything. Karen Lipker, for your help and for everything. Anna, Alex, and Emma Lipker, for being my babies and for three of the four happiest days of my life: the days you were born. Ron Graham, for one of the four happiest days of my life: the day we met. Anne-Marie Cronin, Lisa Michaels-Carrion, Pamela O'Grady, and Viveka von Rosen, for your support, your ear, your challenges, your examples, and your friendship. Kay Kimball for your consistent enthusiasm for life and my life in particular.

Bob Sehlinger, Molly Merkle, Ritchey Halphen, Travis Bryant, Scott McGrew, and everyone at Menasha Ridge Press, past and present, for everything. Diane Stanko-Martinez and Marty Martinez, for true friendship and an example of true love. Mahalo. Geri Kidawski, for your expert Master Naturalist guidance and your friendship. Jen Janssen, for being the absolute best mom and best friend I will ever know. Johnny Molloy, for being a mentor and walking me through your success. Abby Balfany, for being the best neighbor, friend, and lead support staff. Andrew Warnock, for your cute children's book and for the good ideas regarding camping with kids. Laurel School of Arts and Technology, for being a safe, fun place to learn. Having my kids at such a terrific neighborhood school feels is like having an automatic second family. Lindsay Hopper, for taking such good care of baby Emma. Lindsay Smith, for taking such good care of all of my babies. Lisa Eaton, for your ideas and for your enthusiasm for your own books. Michael Bollinger, for being the original unconditional helper.

Renee Putman, Kris Baltrum, and Murielle Watzky-Brewer, for always being there and for your unwavering support. Nancy Stilson-Herzog, for being the Trainer Extraordinaire. Deb Murr and Tanja Pliler, for giving me time at home. Richard Hunt, for the original idea all of those Outdoor Retailer conferences ago. Russell Helms for starting this whole mess and being my favorite Obi-Wan. We are missing you desperately. Susan Cullen Anderson and Jenny Cromie, for your careful look at this important book. Your keen eyes are an essential piece of the package. Susan Haynes, for turning a girl into a woman. You are the perfect editor, and I am so glad you came on board when you did. *Girls Guide* was a good concept, and *Smart & Savvy* is a great book thanks to you.

About the Author

KIM LIPKER grew up in Colorado loving the outdoors from an early age. She is the author of three other guidebooks for Menasha Ridge Press: *60 Hikes with 60 Miles: Denver and Boulder; The Best in Tent Camping: Colorado, 4th Edition* (with Johnny Molloy); and *Day & Overnight Hikes: Rocky Mountain National Park*. She also wrote *The Unofficial Guide to Bed & Breakfasts and Country Inns in the Rockies* (Hungry Minds). In addition to writing books, Kim writes a regular parenting column and other features for *Rocky Mountain Parent Magazine*; for the Web site Away.com, she contributes features, ratings, and reviews covering parks, active sports, and outdoor adventures in the Rocky Mountains and Hawaii.

Kim has been at the writing thing for a while, having had her first news article published at age 12 and later earning a journalism degree from the University of Missouri–Columbia.

Kim lives in Fort Collins, Colorado, with her three children, Anna, Alex, and Emma.

For more information on her upcoming projects, visit her blog at **trekalong.com/lipker.**

Preface

Take a Hike, Girlfriend!

Hiking sounds simple: you walk outside. Certainly when my sister and I were growing up in the mountains of Colorado, we never stopped to put a name to the constant running, walking, and exploring we were doing among all those trees and slopes. We were "playing." Muffin, our adventurous family cat, trailblazed alongside us.

But now that I write outdoor guidebooks for a living, people frequently ask me when I began this way of life. In a radio interview, I told listeners about my earliest memories of hiking a human-made trail. It was in Rocky Mountain National Park, where numbers on posts interpreted points around a lake. Our parents had us stand by those numbers every year to mark our ages. When each of us turned 8, there we were, by number 8 post, on the Bear Lake Trail. And so on.

As a child, I dreaded the time when my outdoor world might be limited, when I would be a grown-up. Instead, hiking became my "work." In fact, it is my calling. Helping women maximize their outdoors potential is my first-aid response to an emergency described by author Richard Louv. His book *Last Child in the Woods: Saving Our Children from Nature-Deficit*

Disorder makes a compelling case that young generations are disconnecting from the natural world, the land, their families, and each other. A noted children's advocate, Louv relates nature-deficit disorder to many kids' increasing depression, distraction, and obesity. Luckily, *Last Child in the Woods* also shows us an alternate future, with families heading back outside. As mothers, wives, partners, grandmothers, sisters, aunts, and friends, we can help make that happen.

As a woman, I am grateful for the gifts that hiking offers me—and my three children. In these pages I have tried to share the joy of my experience with women of all ages. I hiked during all of my pregnancies, and it nourished my body, mind, and soul. Then, after my babies were born, I used the calm of the outdoors to soothe their little spirits. Sections in Part Four (Hit the Trail) and Part Five (For Women Only) cover a lot of ground about hiking with children—in utero and beyond. Part Five also offers straight talk about aging, trail hygiene, and other issues especially significant to women. Part Six, Mama Said There'd Be Days Like This!, covers crucial information about violence and safety. I've included a special section, "Journaling the Journey," to inspire you to use hiking time to sort out your deepest needs and goals.

Throughout, you'll see that hiking is a great way to build relationships—with yourself as well as others. I had to smile when a male friend told me recently that he always wished he had a girlfriend who hiked. I know how he feels. I am often looking for a partner, because matching schedules isn't easy. Making time and taking time (yes, they are different) pose challenges for seasoned hikers and novices alike. You'll find these topics in Part One, in "Strike a Balance."

Thus, *Smart & Savvy Hiking* takes you beyond mere physical exercise, and I have scoped it for beginners, intermediates, and advanced trekkers. Of course, you'll find the nuts and bolts of hiking. (Many tips may surprise women who've racked up hundreds of trail miles under their REI belts). Part Two, Ready! Set! Go!, will help all skill levels shop and plan for maximum comfort and style according to climate, season, and trail terrain. With all the advances in clothing and gear in recent years, we've come a long way from old flannel shirts and sneakers. Fabric and materials can make a crucial difference in whether you enjoy a hike or can't wait to get home.

Ready to venture beyond a short walk or an invigorating day trip? Part Seven, After Sundown, steers you to hard-core trekking and camping. Veteran trailblazers can choose among many epic pilgrimages. Many women make their odysseys on the Continental Divide Trail, Pacific Crest Trail, or Appalachian Trail, as just three examples.

Throughout, *Smart & Savvy Hiking* encourages each woman to follow her own path, literally. If you are new to this activity, start slow! Begin close to home, in familiar environments. That's the best way to guarantee a lifetime relationship with nature. And whether you're a novice or expert, it will never matter whether you travel on park trails, across open country, up rugged mountains, or along city concrete: going by foot is a great way to experience the world.

When Juliette Gordon Low founded the Girl Scouts in 1912, she knew that girls would be attracted to the outdoors for the sports, camping, and nature study. Her vision dispelled the notion of her day that women did nothing more strenuous than "sit on a cushion and sew a fine seam," as early-20th-century poet James Whitcomb Riley described it. I like to think that Mrs. Low herself would be drawn to the title of this book, *Smart & Savvy Hiking: What Every Woman Needs to Know on the Trail.* The word *smart* denotes knowledge and understanding; *savvy* implies practical, up-to-date awareness. You need both on the trail, and I hope that *Smart*

& *Savvy* lives up to its title as a handy tool and life-enrichment device for you.

So take a hike, girlfriend! You go, girl! Get out there and make your footprint on the world.

—*Kim Lipker*
Fort Collins, Colorado

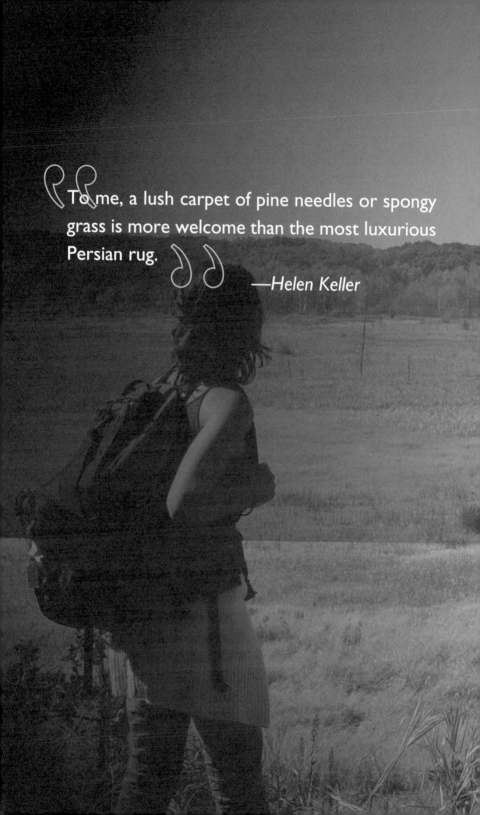

"To me, a lush carpet of pine needles or spongy grass is more welcome than the most luxurious Persian rug."

—Helen Keller

PART ONE

TOP 5

REASONS
to WALK
the WALK

1 Banish Those **Stir-crazy** *Blues*

OUR BODIES NEED SHELTER FROM
THE ELEMENTS, but they also were
made to enjoy the beauty and healing
power of nature. Many indigenous cul-
tures acknowledge this propensity. For
generations, they have embarked on
vision quests—extended periods of
solitude spent in nature for reflection and
guidance. Similarly, the essence of hiking embraces the vision-quest principle
of undistracted time to gain inner direction. Even with a companion, assuming he
or she enjoys peace and quiet, you can
experience hiking as a solitary exercise to
reclaim your own creative spirit.

Unless your work puts you in the outdoors, your day may evolve almost entirely within four walls. You and I both know people who get ready for work, start the car in the garage, drive to the office, park in another garage, take an elevator to the correct floor, and eat lunch at their desk. At quitting time, it's the reverse. These folks may have terrific views of the great outdoors from their windows, especially from the corner office, but they are seldom out in it. In fact, even their exercise time may be inside—at the gym, in a yoga classroom, on a racquetball court.

Perhaps that doesn't describe the exact situation you're in, but it may sound more like your life than you'd like to admit. I know. Even though my work keeps me in nature a lot, I also get caught up in daily demands that take place within heated or air-conditioned rooms. Phones, media, technology, laundry, and bills can imprison all of us.

That's why I think it's useful to compute, from time to time, just how much our lives are divided between indoors and outdoors. Look at it this way: nutritionists often recommend that before starting a diet we record everything we eat over a period of a week or so, to see exactly where the extra calories are sneaking in—and where we may have some bad habits. Likewise, I suggest the simple exercise on page 5 to calculate our indoor–outdoor ratios.

During a typical week, note the hours you spend indoors. Sleep and rest take up a big chunk, of course; then there is the time you're doing household chores, cooking and eating, reading, etc. Tally the time that shopping in stores, work, meetings, and driving a car keep you closed in. (No, having the car windows open does not count as outside time!)

In a separate column, record all of your ventures that let your feet touch earth or pavement. Every minute counts: the time it takes to get the newspaper, to rake the leaves or water the patio plants, to walk the dog, to carry groceries from the store to the car. And, of course, include excursions such as picnics or bike rides. Try to assess how much time you actually feel the sun's rays, the air's chill, or the rain or wind.

At week's end, I bet most of you will reach the same conclusion regarding your outdoors time: an attitude adjustment is in order. Most likely, your tally will make you want to pitch the to-do list out the window and run around in the woods like a little kid!

Unlike us, children have their priorities in order. Given exposure to Mother Nature, they seem to inherently grasp that she is a better teacher than our constructed indoor universe. They instinctively appreciate her natural wonders. My son once told me that his best day ever (one when we were on vacation) was great because he had seen a fish in the waves, a baby turtle struggle through the sand, and the backside of a rather large crocodile.

But let's pause. All of this talk about hiking and getting outdoors sounds good, but is it too much pressure? You're already bombarded daily with ways to be a better friend, mom, daughter, worker bee; how to keep your home healthy, be green, buy organic, or save the world. Whew! How do you squeeze one more thing into the mix?

Well, just by getting outside, we can let nature calm some of those stresses. Hiking offers the physical and mental space to figure out how to manage it all. And it does double-duty in the family-ties, friendship-making departments. Often your best hiking partner is your child, spouse, neighbor, or coworker.

Referring back to the vision quests mentioned earlier, there is a reason that these sacred treks into nature have endured for eons: they work! I believe that hiking can help

Your Indoor–Outdoor Ratio		
Time Spent	Activity (IN, some OUT)	Take It Outside (OUT, some IN)
8 hours	Sleeping	Sleep on the screened porch
2 hours	Cooking	Cook on the grill
2 hours	Eating	Eat at an outdoor cafe
1.5 hours	Laundry	Hang clothes on the line
1.5 hours	Cleaning	Hire cleaning service; go hiking
0.5 hours	Reading mail	Move chair outside
1 hour	Playing with kids	Play outside
0.5 hours	Playing with cat	Play outside
1 hour	Entertaining book club	Meet on the patio
0.5 hours	Dressing	Better keep inside
1.5 hours	Watching TV	Go hiking instead
2 hours	On computer	Take the laptop out on the deck (use an extension cord if needed)
0.5 hours	Walking in park	Keep it up!
0.5 hours	Walking dog	You're already there!
0.5 hours	Baby in stroller	You're still there!
0.5 hours	Gardening	Way to go!
Total hours IN:	22 hours	.5 hour
Total hours OUT:	2 hours	23.5 hours
Total day:	24 hours	24 hours

you clear your mind, reach your potential, make better decisions, and appreciate the mystery of life.

Note: Once you've completed your indoor–outdoor
ratio, hold on to it for an exercise prescribed in "Strike a
Balance" (see page 17).

2 Work Your *Body*

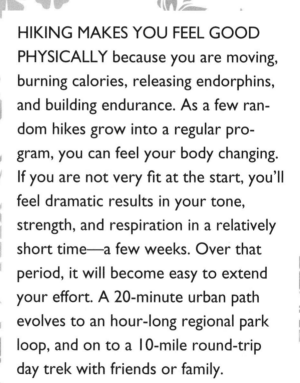

HIKING MAKES YOU FEEL GOOD PHYSICALLY because you are moving, burning calories, releasing endorphins, and building endurance. As a few random hikes grow into a regular program, you can feel your body changing. If you are not very fit at the start, you'll feel dramatic results in your tone, strength, and respiration in a relatively short time—a few weeks. Over that period, it will become easy to extend your effort. A 20-minute urban path evolves to an hour-long regional park loop, and on to a 10-mile round-trip day trek with friends or family.

If you're already in athletic condition, you'll still relish the subtle improvements in your body. You'll be primed to pace yourself faster and faster, and up steeper and steeper terrain. This easy-to-advanced sport also uses different muscle groups from those exercised in other activities. It provides a counterpoint to high-impact pursuits such as jogging, aerobics, and tennis. Certainly hiking is less jarring to your joints than those popular sports.

And I have a special word for those of you dedicated to the poses of Pilates or the *asanas* (movements) of yoga: Combining either of these practices with hiking is a union made in heaven. Both greatly expand the strength and flexibility of your toes, feet, knees, hamstrings, hips, and lower back—all A-team performers during any hike. If your lower-body core is weak, your stride can become imbalanced and strain the whole body.

I have a friend who says that one particular yoga exercise has transformed the way she hikes. She says: "At the start of my yoga class, which happens to be all women, my teacher says, '*Mula bandha,* ladies! Squeeze those vaginas, tighten those perineal muscles, bring your tailbone forward.'

"So what I've noticed," my friend says, "is that when I do this same thing while hiking, it makes me swing my walk better from my hips. I don't lean forward, and I don't help myself with my shoulders trying to get ahead of my knees."

What she describes is a sort of yoga version of the famous Kegel exercise, the one we've heard about from our gynecologists or read about in women's magazines. It tightens the vaginal walls, but more than that, it automatically aligns your posture because it makes you pull in your stomach and straighten your back.

The sly thing about *mula bandha* (Sanskrit for this intimate muscular movement) is that you can practice it on the trail without anyone knowing what you are doing! No one but you will be aware of it. At first, your hikes may feel more arduous, but eventually you'll realize the benefits of stronger legs and a more powerful stride.

Having done Pilates for several years as a cross-training program for all of my outdoor pursuits, I find it improves my posture, breathing, and core strength. I feel like I walk taller and breathe better, thanks to a good balance between hiking and Pilates.

As for yoga, innovative yoga-hiking classes and retreats are popping up nationwide. At first, I wondered what it would be like to do the downward-dog asana in the wilderness. I quickly learned that it is a revitalizing way to deeply inhale fresh air, touch the earth, and appreciate your place in nature. After these hikes, participants typically head indoors for meditation and more yoga. Combining hiking with the healing postures and simple meditation techniques of yoga allows you to expand your self-awareness, mindfulness, compassion, breath, and movement.

You know the common expression that we should "listen to our bodies." But sometimes we may misinterpret the message! Inertia can lead us to believe we are low on energy and need to just sit or lie around. When that happens, it doesn't take much persuasion to cop out on exercise. That novel is a real page-turner? There's a great movie on TV? Hmmm. . . . Yes, I have those days. But if I haven't exercised that day, I know that may be part of my problem. My very best antidote is to take a hike. Sometimes my walk may not be as vigorous as usual because I am a little tired. But that's OK. I just move more slowly, relish the sights and sounds around me, maybe not go as far as I did the day before. I still come back more energized, more clearheaded, and ready to, well, watch that movie I recorded! And I actually enjoy the show even more.

Maybe that's because I feel I "earned" the treat. But I truly think it's because I feel proud of myself, that I pushed myself just a little bit more than I thought I felt like doing. And note my wording here: "more than I *thought* I felt like doing." The culprit was inertia, not really my pep deficit.

I'll also admit that sometimes I've had to force myself to get outdoors. I do that when I feel a cold coming on, and I find that if I can sweat out those germs, I often defeat the virus early on. This can also work for headaches and general aches and pains. Endorphins are miracle workers. And to access those little analgesics, we don't have to run to the pharmacy, fork over cash, or visit the doctor. They all come free in our brains, and we activate them simply by moving our bodies!

This would be a good place for me to rein myself in and issue the disclaimer you've probably been expecting. I don't advocate hiking when you are actually sick. And you should always consult a doctor before embarking on any level of activity more strenuous than you are accustomed to.

All that I've said is anecdotal and based on my own experiences and those of my family, friends, and acquaintances who are trail-addicted. But a lot of proven information backs this up, and it bears repeating. As you would expect, American Hiking Society (**www.americanhiking.org**) champions the health bonuses of my favorite sport. One point that the society makes—as I indicated with my "start slow" entreaty earlier in this book—is that *you don't have to go on a major expedition.* The society cites the American Heart Association's prescription for walking vigorously 30 to 60 minutes, three to four times per week, to achieve myriad benefits. Accordingly, a hiking program can help you

- Lose weight
- Combat osteoporosis
- Lower your risk of heart disease

• Decrease high blood pressure
• Prevent or control diabetes
• Lessen arthritis pain
• Reduce back pain

All right, I am a Pollyanna about the glories of trail rambling. But with groups like the American Heart Association and American Hiking Society on my side, I think you will agree with me: Hiking forges a win–win path to a long and healthy life.

One Step at a Time

According to the U.S. Centers for Disease Control and Prevention, most people reap great health benefits by just walking 10,000 steps a day, several days a week. How do you know when you've walked 10,000 steps? How far is that? To measure, you need an accurate pedometer (see the box on page 99 of Part Four, Hit the Trail.). Not only will a pedometer track your distance, but it's also a great motivator. According to a recent study by the American College of Sports Medicine, participants who used a pedometer increased their daily walking by an average of 2,000 steps. The average person's stride is about 2.5 feet long, so that means a pedometer would increase your distance by 5,000 feet—just 280 feet short of a full mile! (See more about step calculations at **www.thewalkingsite.com/10000steps.html.**)

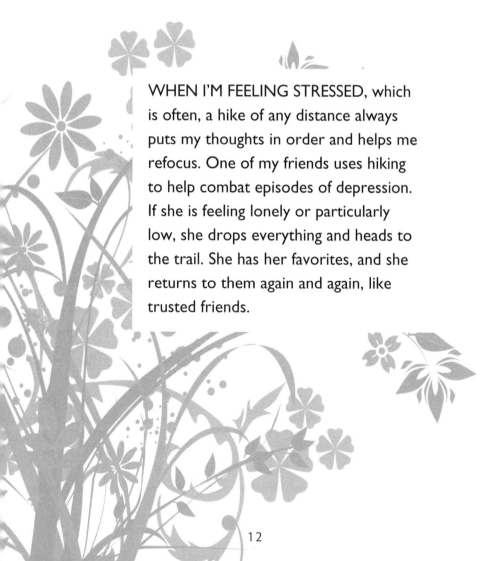

3 *Calm* Your Mind

WHEN I'M FEELING STRESSED, which is often, a hike of any distance always puts my thoughts in order and helps me refocus. One of my friends uses hiking to help combat episodes of depression. If she is feeling lonely or particularly low, she drops everything and heads to the trail. She has her favorites, and she returns to them again and again, like trusted friends.

My refreshed mental clarity and my friend's relief are real, originating from Mother Nature's own chemical supply. According to studies by the American Heart Association (AHA), consistently referenced by American Hiking Society, a walking or hiking program serves mental health by releasing two substances: "calming brain chemicals called endorphins, which are natural tranquilizers; and adrenaline, produced by the body to cope with real or perceived danger." The AHA studies go on to state, "If the adrenaline isn't released from the body, it accumulates, causing muscle tension and feelings of anxiety."

Consequently, if you are going through a life change, the exercise of hiking can function as a form of therapy. Many people I know have used the outdoors, primarily hiking, as a distraction when they have gotten divorced, changed jobs, had babies, moved to a new house, lost a loved one, or watched the kids leave home. It is extremely important to maintain your physical activity during stressful times.

Such "therapy hiking" doesn't have to be in a wooded setting or distant from an urban environment. Another friend spent the early weeks of a new divorce walking the streets and hills of San Francisco up and down, over and over, to and from the city's parks, along Ocean Beach, and bayside in the Marina District. Sometimes she walked all day, by herself. She found the solace she needed just by opening her door and putting her two legs in motion.

I will confess to you that I, too, went through a divorce recently, and believe me, the trails redeemed my spirits. In fact, for me it was while producing this book, so the healing properties of hiking are fresh in my mind as I write these words. In the act of moving through nature, pain seems to melt away, and our confusing and sometimes shattered world tends to make a little more sense.

I have a nonscientific theory about why this is true. While
I wholeheartedly subscribe to the potency of endorphins and
adrenaline, I believe that when you hike, you become a watch-
er and a listener. That in itself is tranquilizing. Unless you are
whizzing along on a trail, hell-bent to get to some finish line,
you can't help but see how busy nature is and how she oper-
ates in tandem: Worker ants march single file on their trail,
back to their colonies; birds construct their twiggy homes, high
up in the branches; squirrels steal away into the brush, bounty
in their cheeks. You feel akin to the thousands of organisms
satisfying their needs for food and shelter. Such observations
remind us that every creature, including each of us, has a place
and a value in this world. That is pretty reassuring.

One way to hold onto the results of a hike's calming
effects is to write about it. I feel so strongly about the power
of this exercise in nature that I've prepared an entire special
section, Journaling the Journey, on page 132. I recommend
carrying a small notebook—not typing out your thoughts on
your iPhone or BlackBerry or other PDA. Used in tandem
with your adventure, a journal can help you

- Express feelings and thoughts
- Find deeper meaning in your life
- Enrich your relationship with yourself, others, and nature
- Define and implement life changes
- Make more conscious choices and decisions
- Sort out challenges in your life

4 Strike a *Balance*

TRUST ME, I KNOW HOW HARD IT CAN BE TO *getthekidstoschooltakecareofthebabydothechoreserrandshavealife. . . .* You know that routine. Sometimes I wish we could buy a guidebook to life—a guidebook like the ones that help us pick hiking trails. We'd know ahead of time which part of our future would be easy or moderate or difficult—or dangerous (that is, Don't Go There!). We wouldn't have to figure it out and often make the wrong choices. But it all boils down to how we use our time. No matter how rich or poor, young or old, married or single, demanding job or not, with children or without—the universal elixir we have is Time (note the capital *T*).

So how do you get started on the path to balance work, play, family, and self on the pommel horse of 24-hour days? Can you use hiking as a tool to harmonize? Like the *micro-hiking goals* I describe in the box on page 23 (and which you can adapt to daily life), this challenge can be broken into doable steps. To me, there are five hurdles to work through.

FIRST HURDLE: *Define Your Goal*

Along with the demands you *must* meet, myriad options probably tempt you. Browsing in the bookstore? Coffee breaks with friends? Boning up on national politics? Playing with your kids? Whatever, you'll have to choose, because as you know, time does not grow on trees. (And you know the joke: no one wants his or her tombstone to read, "I wish I'd spent more time at the office.")

But if your recurring goal is to spend more time outside doing something that clears your mind and works your body, then it sounds to me like you want to take a hike, girlfriend! Decide what really can work for you *now,* and what you aspire to grow into with this program. Maybe all you can imagine right now is a 30-minute stroll at a local park two times a week. But you can envision a daylong excursion in the woods nearly every weekend by next spring. To get there from here means prioritizing, commitment, persistence, and follow-through.

A friend tells her theory about goal-setting that works for anything you want to accomplish: "I'm consistently amazed at women when they talk about winning the lottery," she says. "I simply ask them, 'Do you buy lottery tickets?' and their reply is usually no. How do you win the lottery if you aren't buying lottery tickets?"

The same goes for getting in shape and working your body. You have to be doing something that will lead to your desired result. While purchasing a lottery ticket probably increases your chance of becoming a millionaire by only an infinitesimal degree, you are pretty much guaranteed to emerge from a regular hiking program with much more energy for a balanced life.

SECOND HURDLE:
Go on a Subtraction Diet

From the day we are born, we are running out of time, amortizing ahead of us. So the only way to compete with time is to free some of it up. The most liberating technique for me is what I label the subtraction diet.

You will recall the indoor–outdoor ratio exercise that you completed (didn't you?) from this book's "Banish Those Stir-crazy Blues" section. Take a look at that record of a week's time in your life, and give some hard thought to where your hours go, regardless of whether it's inside or out.

Here's where the subtraction diet comes in: What can you give up, starting now? What can you delegate, outsource, do less perfectly, and eliminate all together? A lot more than you think, I venture to guess.

I don't mind delegating some chores. For example, my 8-year-old may unload the dishwasher with a lot of banging, but at least it's getting done. Right there I'm gaining ten minutes a couple of times a day.

When it comes to "outsourcing," I use the clichéd formula that time is money. It works for me, and I think it will for you, too. Assign a dollar amount to what an hour of your time is worth. In my case, I base the total on the amount of money that I can earn in so many hours and divide it from there. What I can't put a value on is what it costs me to be away from my kids; so I factor that into what I'll gain if I hire someone for chores so I can take them hiking or on other outings they love. For example, it's worth it to me to pay someone $35 for a weekly yard-work session. The dollars pale in comparison to the rewards I reap. So everyone gains—my family, the yardwoman, and me. (Not to mention my yard!)

I have always been a perfectionist, but I finally figured out that if something I am working on is *good enough,* then I need to just stop right there. I've learned that it's better to show up for a dinner party relaxed than to spend frantic hours making the most impressive dessert to bring along. Toning down my perfectionism streak shifts my focus to what's really important. And I'm sorry, but hand-making two dozen favors for my own kid's Poodle in Paris First Birthday Party just isn't crucial. As a friend says, "No one will miss what they didn't know you planned to do!"

Some things can be put off or eliminated altogether. On my own to-do list, I regularly scratch out things that can take a rest, wait till later, or just be deleted. Organizing the holiday wrapping paper may not be as important as recycling your psyche with a dip outdoors. Checking your e-mail every 15 minutes can also wait. Give your cell phone a rest too. Take that hike, girlfriend!

THIRD HURDLE:
Reschedule Your Schedule

Make hiking a *nonnegotiable* calendar item and work other things around it. In fact, say aloud to yourself, "It's nonnegotiable." One of my acquaintances used this technique for her 6 a.m. pre-work swim routine. Whenever she was tempted to linger in her warm bed, or whenever anyone asked her about her fitness program, she would say to herself and to them, "it's nonnegotiable. That's the only way I can stick to it." For her, it was the fear of "this time I won't go" becoming the habit instead of the swim being the habit.

Trust me, a goal will never be realized if it is not assigned a time and place, like a deadline. Even in my work, writing about outdoor adventure, I have a timetable for my outings. No one comes to my door and says, "Hey, Kim, it's time to experience the dream trail you want to put in your book."

If you want to start out with one hike a week, then you need to schedule one hike a week. You have control here, just take it. Make that appointment with yourself. That time slot does not always have to involve the actual hike, as long as you are setting it aside to at least focus on some aspect of your goal. Studying trail guides, ordering maps, and making phone calls to line up companions takes time. Regarding companions, it's a good idea to buddy up with other people; it makes you accountable and gives you a built-in support system and hiking mates.

Author Julia Cameron has a national following for her book *The Artist's Way* and the concept behind it. One of Cameron's key requisites for tapping into our creative potential is to make a weekly appointment with ourselves that she calls "the artist's date." It can be visiting an art gallery or stitching needlepoint, or . . . you know what I'm going to say . . . going for a hike. Whatever and wherever, it is meant to be an inviolable appointment for time alone, to let our minds scamper freely and unleash our natural creativity. In a way, it is like a weekly mini-version of the vision quests I mentioned in "Banish Those Stir-crazy Blues." (I do caution you in various parts of this book to never hike alone. But of course there are many places that you know well, such as local parks and gardens, where you would feel perfectly comfortable walking alone for an "artist's date" with yourself. So I know there are exceptions.)

But I can't overstress the importance of this calendar-noted appointment with yourself. Consider it a deadline—and one that you'll be ready to meet because you will be prepared. Keep your hiking basics ready to go: hiking clothes and shoes or boots; hat and sunglasses; water bottle; sun and insect protection; and relevant guidebooks or maps. (More about these necessities and others in Part Two, Ready! Set! Go!)

Having said all of this, here's an example of how to put one foot in front of the other at home so you can put one foot in front of the other on the trail. Determined to go on one hike this weekend, over the course of a couple of days you

- Check the weather forecast
- Call your best friend to see if she's free on Saturday
- Hire a babysitter
- Get out the trail maps
- Pick a 4-mile hike
- Pack your lunch
- Fill your water bottle
- Grab your ever-ready day pack
- Head out the door

Simple, huh?

FOURTH HURDLE:
Vanquish the Guilt

All of this new scheduling may seem like rainbows and pots of gold, and it can be if you are not prepared for it to come under siege. Many obstacles will jeopardize it—from sick kids to work projects to community needs. But force yourself to at least take one hike every week—even if it is for only ten minutes at a time. When you realize how much anxiety that *not* being able to hike causes you, this little taste of freedom will have you back on track in no time.

If the main time thief is your job, then listen up, worka-holics: it is a common paradox that to stay creative and productive—you must make time for recreation and relax-ation. Skimping on such life balance hurts your overall moti-vation and often leads to procrastination, mistakes, and poor judgment. Devoting more time to what you love, like hiking, will actually boost your overall accomplishment and put zing into your life as a partner, wife, soul mate, parent, friend, mentor, worker—all the things you are. If there is one thing I've learned as a young mom, it is that being a little selfish will keep you from being resentful, burned out, cranky, and depressed. Making time for hiking is a win–win situation for everyone.

FIFTH HURDLE:
Keep Your Motivation Stoked

The luster of anything new in our lives—a hobby, a sport, a pair of designer shoes—can dim after a while. You want to avoid letting your hiking routine become stale and boring. Here are some tips to keep in fresh in your life:

• Identify five destinations within an hour of home for day hikes (and overnights, if you take up backpacking). Make a file on each that includes maps, driving directions, and notes on campsites or area lodging.

• Choose different hiking trails, in different locations.

• Sample each trail in all four seasons to appreciate the subtle and dramatic variations.

• Study up on the wildlife, plant life, and trees that popu-late your hiking areas.

• Become a bird-watcher and start your life list. Buy a birdsong CD and learn to identify the coos and calls that define nature's sopranos.

• Take out-of-town guests to your favorite hiking destinations and see familiar places through their inquisitive eyes.

• Combine hiking with another activity you enjoy, such as fly-fishing or rafting/canoeing/kayaking.

• Learn a new skill, such as how to use handheld global-positioning system (GPS) navigation on your hikes.

• If you take up overnight excursions, walk by day and sleep in a trail hut or cabin, or even pull a tent out of your backpack.

• Hire a guide to get you out into areas where you never thought you would tread.

Final Equation

Summing up, here is the equation I *try* to live by and that I think will add up for you, too: Regular exercise (that is, hiking) + nutritional diet + adequate rest = reduced stress = more energy = readiness for variety in life = perfect balance. *Voilà!*

Micro Hiking, Macro Life

When I've been out all day on a challenging course, I'm tired, and it seems it will take an eternity to walk the last mile, I switch on those *microhiking goals* I mentioned earlier. The technique goes like this. Say I am on a trail with familiar twists and turns. As I march along, I think to myself: Make it to that old aspen tree. Then make it to that big boulder with the moss on top. Then to the KEEP OUR TRAILS CLEAN sign. Say my ABCs. Cross the wooden bridge. From there I will see the car. Then I can have the dark-chocolate bar that's still in my backpack. Now there's a goal worth hiking for! I do love chocolate.

As long as I'm engaging in my goal-setting, it seems that the last mile, or the entire hike, is more manageable. I often apply these microvisualizations to life, and it helps me accomplish tasks or get through situations that seem formidable at the outset. Baby steps, mentally or physically, can help you cover huge distances.

5 Become *Nature's* Steward

AMONG THE MILLIONS OF WORDS penned by the late Rachel Carson are these thought-provokers for your next walk or hike: "One way to open your eyes is to ask yourself, 'What if I had never seen this before? What if I knew I would never see it again?' " Such reflection increases our awareness of the world, and fosters our desire to care for the environment.

Obviously Carson knew that. Born in Pennsylvania in 1907 and raised on a simple homestead, this renowned author, scientist, and conservationist grew up at a time when plunder of the countryside was rampant in the name of "progress." But Carson herself was nurtured by her nature-loving mother and the mesmerizing beauty of their Allegheny River surroundings. Consequently, she became a trailblazer—literally—in the name of nature. (Every June, the Rachel Carson Trails Conservancy sponsors a 34-mile, one-day endurance hike on what the conservancy calls the "brutal Rachel Carson Trail." Visit **www.rachelcarsontrails.org/rct/challenge** if you're feeling peppy.)

All of this makes me aware of the effects of nature on our souls—and on our children. I keep coming back to my son's eloquent realization, mentioned in the "Banish Those Stir-crazy Blues" section of this book. He recalled the happiest day of his life (thus far) as the time he had witnessed the fish, turtle, and crocodile all in their natural habitats on our vacation. He may never forget that day, and he may look back on it as a turning point in his life. We never know what lasting influence the exposure to nature can have on our kids. Or our nieces and nephews, our friends' kids, and all the younger generations that we have a chance to take along on some of our hikes. We never know where it will lead. Perhaps one of them will be the next Rachel Carson.

To encourage children in nature, a local author and friend of mine, Andrew Warnock, wrote an outdoor science book called *Trouble in the Rubble!* Andrew says that simple items like a pocket microscope, binoculars, and tree-finder books are great to bring along on a hike with kids. To sharpen their observation skills, he encourages them to count legs on bugs, look for sparkly minerals in rocks, note shapes in clouds, and really listen to bird songs. At a stream, he has them sort pebbles by color, and he gets them to collect pinecones with different shapes.

My point is that hiking is a fabulous way to explore and learn to care for the environment. Appreciating wildlife is not merely the act of identifying a moose, or a deer, or a crab. Most importantly, it is developing a basic awareness of ecology, or how plants and animals (including us) fit together in Earth's natural systems. You may not be a scientist, but hiking through different habitats and climate zones helps develop a scientist's curiosity. We can't help but notice changes that compromise the existence of plants and nonhuman animals. They are warning signs of global warming and other conditions that affect our human survival as well.

For example, you may remark to your companion that fewer birds seem to be migrating through an area than in past winters. Or that the tree line has moved slightly higher than it was a few years ago when you brought the kids here. Or that mountain lions have moved into an area you can no longer feel safe in. Such ecological shifts remind us of Rachel Carson's foreboding questions.

As residents of Planet Earth, our "environmental eye" is the prism to understand how all living things interrelate, and how to use and enjoy natural resources with minimal impact on the land. With today's (thank goodness) emphasis on conservation and the Green Movement, a lifelong outdoors person like me is lucky to have had these sensibilities woven throughout my core from childhood. When we care about, value, respect, and love nature, then others we touch will adopt our awe.

For *all of us,* I write this book. And for you, I say, "Way to go, girl!" You didn't realize that, by hiking, you may be saving the world.

Adventure is worthwhile in itself.
—Amelia Earhart

PART TWO

READY!

SET!

GO!

Planned *Spontaneity*

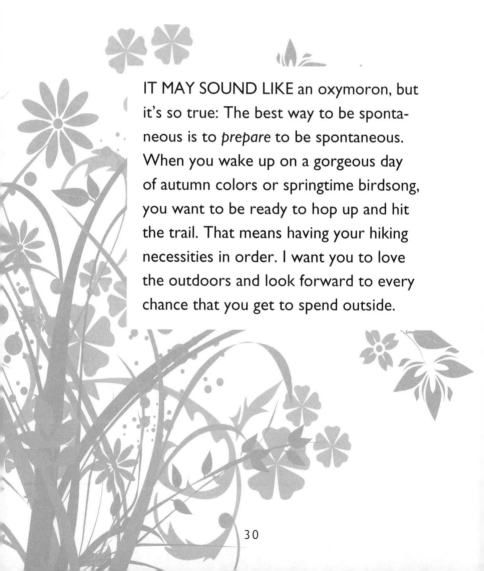

IT MAY SOUND LIKE an oxymoron, but it's so true: The best way to be spontaneous is to *prepare* to be spontaneous. When you wake up on a gorgeous day of autumn colors or springtime birdsong, you want to be ready to hop up and hit the trail. That means having your hiking necessities in order. I want you to love the outdoors and look forward to every chance that you get to spend outside.

Unfortunately, I've known many women who came back from their outings full of troubles. They were covered in mosquito bites. They were cold, tired, and hungry. They had gotten lost or hiked trails that were too long. Their companions complained nonstop. They didn't have enough water. It rained. It snowed. It was too hot. How dreary for everyone!

It doesn't have to be that way. Yes, you may get a blister (despite your best efforts at proper shoe fit). You may have a hangnail (I always do!). Your boots may be caked with mud (they will shine again). You may be sweaty (you'll clean up nicely). But those problems don't offset an otherwise great experience that you were ready to take on.

Pick *the* **Place**

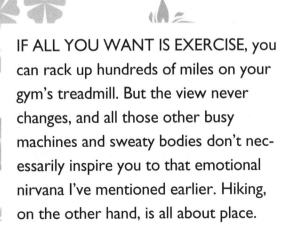

IF ALL YOU WANT IS EXERCISE, you can rack up hundreds of miles on your gym's treadmill. But the view never changes, and all those other busy machines and sweaty bodies don't necessarily inspire you to that emotional nirvana I've mentioned earlier. Hiking, on the other hand, is all about place.

You can choose among hundreds of hiking environments, limited only by your imagination and where you need to travel. Most hiking guidebooks give trail recommendations or include a quick reference on the best hikes in the region. Within the first few pages of my books, I usually break down the hikes into these categories: summit, historic, lake, river, waterfall, meadow, above tree line, best for children, loop, by mileage, and by difficulty.

Perhaps I am so gung ho about this sport because I live within a few hours of prairie, mountains, wilderness, timberline and above, woods, rivers, sand dunes, and more. I can hike on urban trails and in nature preserves, county open space, state parks, U.S. Forest Service and Bureau of Land Management lands, national parks, and more. *Whew!*

Depending on your home base, you also may have many options. Sometimes such bounty can keep you from actually getting out the door, due to indecision. An acquaintance of mine lives in an urban area featured in one of the *60 Hikes within 60 Miles* series produced by (full disclosure here) my publisher, Menasha Ridge Press. In her Deep South town, and at the end of a hot summer, this woman wasted the entire first cool Sunday studying all the hikes in the book. Pretty soon, it was dark outside! So there is a lot to be said for Just Doing It. Still, it does pay to carefully select your hiking destination.

As a practical matter, in your own area you'll know if you're better off on the botanical gardens path that meanders around a peaceful lake or on the hilly and densely forested regional park trail. But for pathways you've heard less about, you can almost always get the basics about a trail's terrain in a guidebook for the area or region, or on a Web site that includes a specific trail's information. One handy resource is **Trails.com,** which has detailed descriptions and maps of some 43,000 trails across the United States. (As of press time, membership dues for unlimited access to the site are $49 per year, but you can click on its standing 14-day free trial subscription.)

Most importantly, you need to find a path that is *within your ability*. Fortunately or unfortunately, hiking trails have no equivalent to American Whitewater's International Scale of River Difficulty used by the rafting community. That scale rates rapids as Class I (easy), II (novice), III (intermediate), IV (advanced), V (expert), and VI (extreme and exploratory—that is, very dangerous). The reason I say "fortunately" is that we have no equivalent scale—hiking is not the archetype of high-risk adventure and perhaps does not require rigorous classifications. (While there are dangers to be aware of, as detailed in Part Six of this book, on a typical hike you can always turn back if the trail starts to look too steep or rocky or simply is not to your liking.) On the other hand, I say "unfortunately," because it would surely help to have some national data bank, kept current for every trail in America!

So we rely on regional guidebooks that most often show-case key information for each trail in some type of box or screened sidebar. When you're choosing a trails guidebook, this is the kind of information that will be most helpful for you, particularly if you are not familiar with the area and/or you are new to hiking. So I would suggest looking over that information before you purchase the book.

For example, in some hiking guides I've authored, the publishing-house style calls for "Key At-a-Glance Information" that simply gives the trail's location, its length, and whether it is easy, moderate, or difficult. That may be all you want. But in other guides, the publisher requires me to provide a more comprehensive profile box, as shown in the example on the next page.

The following excerpt from my book *Day & Overnight Hikes: Rocky Mountain National Park* (Menasha Ridge Press, 2008) describes in a nutshell the Cow Creek Trailhead for Bridal Veil Falls. My ratings are based on the publisher's **five-star system;** except for the absolute calculation of the geographic distance, it relies on my own observations and personal experience.

SCENERY: ★★★★ (By four stars, I indicate that it is very picturesque, but not as awesome as a five-star-scenery hike would be.)

TRAIL CONDITION: ★★★★ (Four stars means it's very good. By comparison, one star would indicate it's rocky, overgrown, or otherwise not so appealing.)

CHILDREN: ★★★ (This rating tells you that I think able-bodied children would enjoy it.)

DIFFICULTY: ★★★ (You can plan on this trail being moderately difficult, right in the middle between very easy—at one star, and very arduous—at five stars.)

SOLITUDE: ★★★ (With one star indicating it's a tourist attraction and five stars denoting that it will be you and your companions and the wildlife, this is well-balanced for quiet time, but not isolated.)

DISTANCE: 6.4 miles out-and-back (It's not 6.3 miles or 6.5 miles; it is 6.4 miles to the tenth measured by GPS!)

EXPECTED HIKING TIME: 3.5 hours (I calculated a pace of 2 to 3 mph, with time for taking pictures, or writing a page in your journal, or having that chocolate bar while gazing from the overlook.)

OUTSTANDING FEATURES: Thundering waterfall; meadow and alpine landscape; historical ranch. (These elements speak for themselves!)

As you can see, "a hike is a hike is a hike" is just not the case. Many different outdoor scenarios await to be the perfect one for you today, or next weekend, or whatever your time frame happens to be. Your own needs and desires are dynamic and ever-changing: How much time do you have for the activity today? How energetic do you feel? What would work for your hiking companion(s)? And what are you in the mood for? Is it simply to hike, or do you want to make the excursion more engaging or meaningful? Is this a bird-watching trip? A first double-digit miles hike?

Of course weather, altitude, and possible hazards influence your choices as well. Maybe the forecast is for heavy rain in the area you had counted on, so you get out the guidebook and pinpoint another spot. Maybe you're on vacation in a higher altitude than you are accustomed to. In that case, you should drink lots of water, abstain from alcohol, and avoid pushing yourself too hard until your body is acclimated. As for hazards, in bear or wildcat country, for example, you should take all of the precautions described in Part Six, Mama Said There'd Be Days Like This!, on page 164.

Most importantly, you must be honest with yourself as to your physical capabilities. Keep progression in mind as you begin hiking. It's better to start with a simple walk around your neighborhood or a stroll in the park before tackling a full-day hike. There is a big difference between a three-hour walk on an easy one-star trail versus a three-hour trek on a strenuous five-star trek. Or a three-hour hike on a well-maintained (four-star) trail compared with the same time spent on a one-star overgrown path where you can lose your bearings. So you have to weigh all of the factors together.

I've said it before in Part One, and you've heard it a million times, but I'll say it again: If hiking is a new activity for you, please consult a physician before jumping into it. It is a matter of safety, not only for yourself but also for the consideration and peace of mind of your hiking companion(s).

Trail-selection Checklist

You can get most of the information cited below in guidebooks or by calling the visitor center, ranger's office or, in municipalities, the parks and recreation department. Sometimes, however, such resources don't know about the sign posted yesterday at the site. Perhaps a giant eucalyptus tree was uprooted and toppled in a storm last week, blocking your intended trail. It pays to have an alternate trail or destination in mind, if you have time to change course. But here are the basics to keep you from overlooking anything in your planning.

❑ Are there facilities at the trailhead? These include parking areas, restrooms, a water supply, trail maps, and a land-line phone.

❑ Is there a kiosk for trail maps? Of course you have the map from your guidebook or Web site printout, but it's *always* a good idea to have a second map source. I recommend eagle-eyeing your trail on both maps and noting any discrepancies before you leave the trailhead. And don't stick the map in your backpack and forget it; reference it often on your journey.

❑ Does the terrain change on your trail during different seasons? Is it flooded or snowed in at certain times of the year?

❑ Are there any local hazards posted, such as deer-tick infestations or mountain-lion sightings?

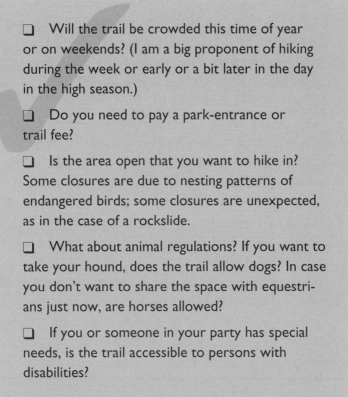

❏ Will the trail be crowded this time of year or on weekends? (I am a big proponent of hiking during the week or early or a bit later in the day in the high season.)

❏ Do you need to pay a park-entrance or trail fee?

❏ Is the area open that you want to hike in? Some closures are due to nesting patterns of endangered birds; some closures are unexpected, as in the case of a rockslide.

❏ What about animal regulations? If you want to take your hound, does the trail allow dogs? In case you don't want to share the space with equestrians just now, are horses allowed?

❏ If you or someone in your party has special needs, is the trail accessible to persons with disabilities?

And, finally, to repeat my earlier cautions:

Consider how you and your hiking buddies are feeling the day of the hike. Is anyone coming down with a cold or other physical ailment?

Calculate how many hours you plan to be on the trail. As mentioned, most hike durations in my guidebooks are based on a 2- to 3-mph average, allowing times for stops and lunch or snacks. For difficult and steep hikes, I adjust this back to 1 to 2 mph.

One of my own hiking partners has type 1 diabetes and is very active. I would rate her as an expert hiker, but I only do so knowing that she takes every precaution before we head out. In her pack are the supplies she needs, including test kits and extra foods and juices. She knows when to stop and say: "I need a rest."

Once you've decided what kind of hike you want to take, check with local parks departments and look at regional maps. As noted in "Got Maps?," on page 65, these maps can come from local, state, county, city, and federal agencies; national parks; and national monuments—you have a world of choices. Of course, your geographic proximity to beaches, mountains, rivers, sand dunes, and other terrain will help dictate those choices.

Be sure you know how much time it takes to get from your door to the trailhead. If you plan to travel an hour in the car, will you be too lethargic to hike? (Sometimes nothing diffuses lethargy like some good exercise.) Do you want to do a loop hike or an out-and-back hike? A loop hike is one that follows a circular pattern; a balloon hike goes out and back along with an additional circular pattern; an out-and-back hike goes to a destination and traces back from there, following the same path.

Shuttle hikes—usually particularly long or strenuous routes—require you to arrange for pickup at the other end of the trail, or to park a second car there. Some hikes include caravans that transport your luggage to a spiffy bed-and-breakfast or inn and you can hike from inn to inn. This is the non-backpacker's ideal—adventure with a soft pillow.

Before you embark on any trail, make sure to tell someone where you will be going. Write down the trailhead, approximate trail route, and when you expect to return. Also, write down who you are going with.

If you are traveling and staying in a hotel or resort, make sure the front desk and/or concierge knows your plan. I suggest you ask them to give your room a call at a certain time just to be sure you are back safely.

Ditto for campground-safety etiquette. Alert a staff member at the visitor center or the ranger's office, or even a neighboring camper—a great way to strike up a new friendship. Or, if it's more comfortable for you, just let a friend or family member back home know your general hiking plans while you are camping; commit to calling or e-mailing them at a certain day or time to assure them that you are accounted for. Don't forget to give them the phone number of the campground headquarters, park visitor center, or ranger's office in case they haven't heard from you by the appointed time.

Let's assume that if you are late to return, it's only because you lingered longer at the once-in-a-lifetime sunset from the mountain peak, or that the waterfall inspired you to write 20 pages in your journal. But underlying all of these suggestions is my motto: "Nature can be very unforgiving, and if you leave word of where you will be, it will be easier for you to stay found."

Go *Shopping*!

TWO POPULAR SEMINARS that relate to women's wear took place at a recent Outdoor Retailer Show. This is the huge trade exhibition that attracts 20,000-plus outfitters and expedition gurus from all over the world to Salt Lake City twice a year—every January and August.

One topic was "The Female Race—How to Design Like a Girl." Speakers Yvonne Lin and Whitney Hopkins ought to know. Both from Femme Den–Smart Design, based in New York City, they put their creative genius to work every day to answer such questions as, "If you're a woman, where are the chest straps supposed to go on backpacks?" (For more on this innovative group, visit **www.femmeden.com.**)

Talking about outdoor clothing and gear for women, Lin echoes the thoughts of most of my fellow hikers when she says, "*Shrink it* and *pink it* are not the way to go! Women are saying, 'I want to look cute doing my sport, but I also want to kick butt! And I don't want to be condescended to.' "

The other session relevant to women's sport clothes was "Color Trends—What's Next & How Do We Know," featuring Leatrice Eiseman. As the author of seven books on color and head of the Eiseman Center for Color Information and Training, she is widely respected for her studies of the effects of color on our product selections. While our gender has no proprietary claim to hue, it is something that we definitely discuss and think about a lot, and color often influences our choice of clothing. In her book *Pantone Guide to Communicating with Color,* Eiseman explains that red shades can produce physical effects, such as a boost in the flow of adrenaline. That could help on the trail. Red hiking boots, anyone? Or maybe some fire-engine-red sunglass frames?

What *you* like to wear on your hike will largely depend on the climate and your location. Wherever that may be, you'll also need to prepare for changes in weather during your trail time. The primary goals when dressing for your hike are fourfold: to stay dry; to keep your temperature at a comfortable level; to protect your skin from intrusions such as sunburn, bug bites, and poisonous plants; and to maintain comfort. That's a lot to think about—as opposed to throwing on a pair of jeans and T-shirt and heading out the door.

IT'S ALL *about* LAYERS

In this discussion of attire, I am tempted to work from the bottom up, because foot care is the number-one consideration for hikers. Or I could go from the top down, because hats are so important for warmth and sun protection. But I think I'll start in the middle. That's where the most fun is, and that's primarily due to all the layers we need, and choices we have.

One of the nice things about modern outerwear is that so much protection is woven into lightweight fabrics that it's easier than ever to layer up and down as temperature, wind, and your exposure fluctuate during a single hike. I have girlfriends who chill when the thermometer dips below 70°F. Others perspire from exertion even in much lower temperatures. Whether you are cold- or warm-natured, in dressing for your hike you should think of three comfort zones:

• Base layer
• Insulation (middle) layer
• Outer (shell) layer

The **base layer** keeps you dry as you alternately sweat and cool during your exercise. Most base-layer garments are made of polyester blends that wick perspiration dampness. This means that they repel moisture away from your skin to the outer portion of the fabric where it can evaporate. Otherwise, you can become chilled from trapped perspiration. Examples of popular brand-name synthetics for all outdoor clothing, including the base layer, are CoolMax, Polartec, and Patagonia's Capilene. Natural fabrics such as thin wool blends or silk are also options for your base layer. *But try to avoid cotton.* Cotton retains moisture and can make you feel cold and wet from your own sweat, even if your outer garments protect you from the elements.

For women, the base layer includes panties and bras or camisoles, as well as long underwear (though sometimes fashion tights can do double duty as long johns). Undies can be loose-fitting for hot weather or snug for more range of motion or to allow for more layering. Leave the skimpy lace panties in their drawer. Instead, choose garments that are comfortable, breathable, and that don't trap odors.

While hiking, the last things you want to deal with are crotch creep and falling or pinching bra straps. For panties, go for higher-cut styles to aid with leg stride and ride-up. For bras, choose those with few seams and minimal hardware on the shoulder area to avoid potential irritation and discomfort with backpack straps.

Thermal underwear is a wise choice for cold seasons or climates. Items are available in light, medium, and heavy/ expedition weights. (If you plan on a walk around the North Pole, you may want the latter.) Fabrics range from luxurious-feeling silks to practical synthetics. If you plan on a variety of hiking activities and climates, your outdoor wardrobe may include a couple of pairs of long johns for different needs.

The **middle layer** is your insulation, charged with keeping your body temperature stable and not in constant battle with the outside air. (Of course, if you are hiking in dry, warm conditions, this may become your outer layer, as you might not want further protection. But in most cases, you will still need at least one more layer, light though it may be, to get your through the variable day.)

The middle layer is the mainstay of your outfit—your hiking pants (or shorts) and shirt. Here again, you will want fabrics that trap air to maintain stable body temperature but that also include wicking properties to keep you dry. Many manufactured fibers have the added qualities of built-in water resistance, a sun-protection factor (SPF), and insect repellent—or some combination of those properties. ExOfficio, for example, manufactures a line of Insect Shield clothing that not only protects you against mosquitoes and other arthropods but also includes an SPF (the protection lasts for 70 washings or so).

Although shorts are a perfect option for hot climates, make sure that you protect your skin from sun exposure, insect bites, and potentially poisonous plants. The perfect choice is convertible or zip-off pants that easily transform from long pants to shorts or vice versa. Because they are so ideal for this sport, some brands are even sold as "hiking pants" or "trail pants." You can tuck the zipped-off bottoms into a little zippered compartment on the pants or into your day pack or backpack. (To avoid zipper rage on the trail, be sure these devices are working properly on each leg before you leave home.)

A similar option is pants with tabs that button to hold the rolled-up leg, so you can turn a pair of long pants into Capri length. For traveling, all styles of convertible pants make for efficient packing in your suitcase and give you two built-in options at your destination.

Any pant you choose should be roomy enough to allow a range of movement and to fit over long johns or tights if needed. Some hiking pants feature elastic waistbands or built-in belts; this helps you avoid uncomfortable external belts and loops under your pack. Styles with tapered ankles or zippers up the legs make it easy to accommodate hiking boots. Other pant features to consider for comfort and convenience include articulated knee areas and several pockets with snap, zipper, or Velcro closures.

For hiking shirts, you know the drill now: look for fabrics that trap air to maintain body heat but that also include wicking properties to keep you dry. That pretty much rules out cotton, once again, in favor of synthetics. As with pants, you'll find several companies offer shirts that have water resistance, insect protection, and/or an SPF incorporated into the fabric. Among many styles, the most convenient is a convertible shirt, similar to the pants described above. You can go long-sleeved when it's cool; then, when you get warm, just roll up the sleeves and fasten them with the self-tab. In warm or hot seasons or climates, you would skip to the outer layer for wind and rain protection if needed. In cool seasons or climates, an additional round of clothing will still count as your middle or insulating layer, along with your shirt and pants.

With chilly or frigid air, wear a vest, sweater, or jacket over your shirt—and be prepared to shed this item into your backpack or tie it around your waist as the day heats up. Good choices are natural fibers such as wool or—only when no rain is forecast—goose down. Fleece, a wool-like synthetic, is probably the most popular insulator and it comes in light, medium, and heavy/expedition weights. Fleece offers myriad advantages: it dries quickly and it is breathable and generally light enough to tie around your waist or stuff into your pack when you need to de-layer. Fleece is also very protective against biting winds.

The **outer layer,** also called the shell layer, is an article dedicated to protection from rain, snow, and wind.

Breathable waterproof shells are particularly well suited for wet weather and cold climates. Because they are breathable, they keep water out, but let vapor through, so you stay warm and dry. Fabrics include a coating, or a laminated membrane such as GORE-TEX. If you plan to get a lot of use from such outerwear, the purchase price of these shells can be more than worth it.

Nonbreathable waterproof shells can keep the rain out, but they tend to be suffocating and will leave you feeling hot and damp unless a ventilation system is built into the garment. Typically made of a durable polyurethane nylon, they're generally cheaper than the breathable alternative.

Water-resistant clothing is not necessarily *waterproof,* so there is no guarantee that it will keep you dry. However, water-resistant breathable shells are a perfect, reasonably priced choice for high-activity hikes in mild climates with limited rainfall. The tightly woven fabric with a water-repelling outer finish effectively keeps wind and cold at bay.

Another choice for outerwear is a jacket or vest that combines insulation with an outer shell—two of your layers in one. Sometimes referred to as soft shells, they can be wind- and water-resistant as well as breathable. Another advantage: There are many versions of this type of garment. You can select one designed for crisp fall days, and another for really cold winter months.

HATS *and* GLOVES *on*

Insulating your head and hands on your hike can make the difference between a miserable, teeth-chattering experience and an invigorating cold-weather adventure.

Without a hat, about one-third of your body heat is lost. So, in cool or cold weather, a wool or fleece hat is one of your most important hiking tools. And year-round, you need a hat to protect against sun exposure. A broad-brimmed style, particularly with a neck shield, provides optimal protection. But a baseball cap will do just fine. (Be sure to put sunscreen on your exposed neck, however.) A drawstring under your chin is also a nice option, especially in windy areas. As with other hiking attire, many hats come with SPF and/or waterproof or water-resistant properties.

And don't forget your gloves. You have many things to do with your arms and hands on a hike—swing them for a vigorous walk, hold your child's hand, make notes in your journal. You don't want be immobilized because your hands are shoved into your pockets to keep warm. Just make sure your gloves fit comfortably. You'll want plenty of dexterity when and if you need to grab or climb unexpectedly.

You can also layer your head and hands for warmth and wind protection: Pull up the hood on your shell jacket before you don your hat. And slip on liners or base gloves to wear underneath your heavier gloves.

And here's a little trick I've learned: sometimes if I've grown cold on the trail and don't feel like adding a sweater or vest from my backpack, I just pop a hat on my head and a pair of gloves on my hands. Miraculously, the rest of my body starts to feel warm again. So a warm head and hands can be efficient transmitters of comfort to the rest of your body.

CHANGE—But Don't Shortchange— YOUR SOCKS

If I had to bet on the one item in your hiking wardrobe that might get dismissive treatment, it would be the socks. And that would be a mistake. Your feet will perspire on a hike, and warmer temperatures and long and strenuous treks will make them even sweatier. Socks that wick away moisture while keeping your feet dry and blister-free is the difference between a miserable, blister-plagued hiker and a happy hiker.

So, since you are putting some considerable time and money into a nice and comfortable pair of boots (see page

49), why not spend a few extra moments and dollars on the right socks? You have considerable choices among both natural and synthetic fibers. Naturally speaking, silk is a great option for liners to go under your main socks. Liners fit snugly to your feet and wick away moisture. Wool socks on top then insulate and keep your skin warm and dry.

Another benefit to liners is that they (rather than your bare skin) rub against the outer sock and thus reduce the chance of blisters. The outer sock you wear with liners will serve as insulation and cushioning. One useful product now on the market is specifically made for hiking: socks with extra cushioning behind the heel and/or under the foot.

When it comes to natural products, try to stay away from cotton unless you are taking a quick walk. Although light and cool, cotton soaks up moisture and is not a good choice for a long hike. Cotton just doesn't make it these days, with so many temperature- and activity-savvy materials for outerwear. As with the other layers you'll be wearing, synthetic-fiber socks wick away moisture, keep your skin dry, and regulate temperature. The lightest and strongest synthetic fiber used for socks is nylon. Spandex is often combined with other materials to give the fabric a snug fit. Polypropylene is light and the best fabric for wicking away moisture from skin, but tends to be stinky and hold onto odors. Brand-name fibers such as Thermax and CoolMax were created by modifying fibers to provide varying degrees of wicking and insulation. Some popular sock brands to consider are SmartWool, Wigwam, and Eagle Mills.

I always suggest that you prep your socks for hiking: wash and wear them a few times, with your hiking boots, before you venture out on an hours-long expedition. And always carry an extra pair of socks in your pack in case you need relief from sweaty or tired feet.

BOOTS

It is impossible to walk far if your feet are compromised. After all, they are your most important hiking tools, and they get pounded by the ground below and by the weight of your body and your gear. Factor in nature's elements and the particulars of your hike, and these tools are in for a beating. As an active hiker, I have been in the doctor's office for plenty of foot-related complaints, including infected hangnails. In between hikes, I baby my feet. They always deserve comfortable shoes for casual and dressy times, and lots of hiking gives me a good excuse for pedicures. (I can feel you scheduling your appointment right now.)

While occasional hiking in athletic shoes isn't a crime, here's an excellent reason to invest in boots: the embarrassment factor. One acquaintance wore her tennis shoes on a hike and encountered a typical summer shower, which of course made the leaves on a very busy trail damp and slippery. You guessed it: she ended up flat on her face in the mud, in front of her loved ones and several strangers. And she got to walk a good 3 miles in those muddy clothes, with scraped and bloody palms, knees, and elbows. After that trip, she followed my advice on hiking boots *and* first-aid kits.

Many people ask what they should spend on a good pair of boots. You've probably guessed by now that I don't believe in skimping on the cost of high-quality boots. But my general response is that all feet are made differently, as are all boots. I always suggest trying on diverse types of hiking footwear, and in several stores—preferably outdoor retailers rather than regular shoe or department stores. Get professional retail advice if you need it, but *never* get pressured into buying a pair of boots that you don't actually love. I believe in building a long and happy marriage between your feet and your hiking boots.

Lightweight boots or hiking shoes are fine for most hiking in good weather. Leather boots are heavier, but they are your best choice for all-round, long-lasting protection and support. Leather also keeps snow and rain from soaking through your boots, to your socks, and then to your feet.

So I recommend leather for most hiking, though you can stay away from boots made for hard winter travel unless you will be conquering hard-core mountaineering. Leather also tends to last longer with proper care, will conform to your feet, and it can be treated with additional waterproofing products.

Most boots rise above the ankle to give support and also have a scree collar to keep out the elements and protect your Achilles tendon. Soles should grip, even on the most slippery surfaces. The fewer the seams, the drier the boot will stay. Pull the tongue flap forward and check to see if the boot's underlying fitting would still keep water out.

When you try on boots, make sure you do so with the socks you intend to wear with them. You may even want to have a really heavy pair for arduous, cold-weather hiking and a thinner pair for lighter, warmer-weather hiking. Bring both pairs to the tryout.

With your socks on, lace the boots up fully and correctly for your comfort. Then you can judge the boot fit by using the finger test: If you can insert at least one finger, but no more than two, between the boot neck and your Achilles tendon, where your calf meets your heel, you have enough room.

During this exercise, keep in mind that terrain, weather, and other conditions all affect how your feet will respond in your boots. Your feet *will* perspire and swell while hiking. A long downhill trek may thrust your toes to the front; side-hill hikes can put pressure on the sides of your feet; and heat buildup can make your feet tender and sore, leading to blisters or "hot spots." To accommodate such factors, in addition to your sock thickness, you may need to go up a half-size from your street shoes. In fact, some hikers' feet expand an entire size while they are on the trail!

With what seems like the right size boot on, walk around. One reason to shop for boots in outdoors retailers rather than regular shoe shops or shoe departments is that many now have incline ramps and replica mini–hiking paths available for test-walking. With or without such assistance, clomp around in the store, up any steps available, on carpeting and off, and over doorway thresholds—anything to get surface variance. As you walk, your heels should not slip and your toes should have wiggle room. I repeat what I said earlier: *never* buy a pair of hiking boots that you don't love!

But once you have lit on the perfect pair, there's still work to do before you hit the trail. Wear them around the house and even on a few errands so they can adjust to the shape of your feet. (If you feel silly in the grocery line, just smile and ignore the stares.)

On these trial walks, note where any trouble spots may be forming, particularly if you already have corns or calluses. You may need to add a foot-care shield or strip, or Band-Aids, or moleskin, or even duct tape to prevent a nasty blister. Sometimes the boot will just take a bit of getting used to, and the proverbial Band-Aid solution is temporary. Other times, you may need to be sure you add the protection to your feet each time you set out.

Sturdy hiking boots can be expensive, but they will last a long time with proper care. Brush off mud and dirt from your boots after each outing. Intense heat can harm leather, so never put your boots too close to the fireplace or a campfire. If they get damp or wet, let them dry in the sun. Every few weeks or months, depending on how often you

Don't Leave Home without 'Em

Sunscreen, sun stick, lip balm with SPF, sunglasses, and insect repellent are just as important to have on a hike as the clothes on your back. You already know that too much exposure to the sun can be cancer-causing and life-threatening, and sunburn is an easy hazard to avoid.

While you may want to put on a base layer of sun-screen while you are dressing (to get it over with and not have to deal with it first thing outdoors), you'll still need a supply of it for touch-up on the trail.

To keep my eyes protected, I always have spare sun-glasses in my pack in addition to the ones perched on my nose or pushed up on my hair. That's because it's really easy to lose a pair on the trail, or sit down on them during your lunch break, or whatever.

The sun stick is a miraculous invention for sun and wind protection: like a deodorant stick, you can quickly apply it to your lips, under your eyes, your nose, your forehead, the backs of your hands—all those exposed areas that start to chafe in the wind or need a sunscreen refresher. I also use sun sticks to treat hot spots midhike, though a friend was appalled when I applied the stick to my heel and then my lips and nose. She asked if I could at least change the order, and I told her that it didn't really matter since I'd be using it again and again! Sun sticks are so easy to carry, I'm never without mine. (One of my friends had never heard of such a product, but when she Googled "sun stick," dozens of sites came up with all sorts of choices—SPFs from 15 to 35, prices from $4 to $20-plus. I think it changed her life!)

In most outdoor settings, you should be sure to have a good insect repellent at all times. (A repellent-and-sunscreen combo is another of my favorite products.) I recommend that you apply creams or lotions to your skin while you are dressing for the hike, then carry a refresher in your pack.

If you prefer sprays, you should do that outside rather than in your house or car. In highly bug-prone areas, particularly with mosquitoes, I like repellents with a high DEET content, such as REI's 98.11% DEET Jungle Juice. Because of its chemical makeup and possible health risks, DEET is something you'll want to apply sparingly to your skin. Better yet, spray it on your clothing, particularly around your pants legs, socks, and shoes. *Note:* Jungle Juice will stain fabrics until the next detergent washing.

I also find towelettes—the ones with insect repellent and others with insect-bite antiseptic—to be convenient for touch-up and bite relief on the trail.

hike, treat the leather with an oil or wax dressing to keep the leather flexible and more water repellent. One of my hiking friends gives her boots a professional "spa treatment" from time to time, taking them to her local shoe-repair shop for a professional cleaning and polishing.

Gear Up:
The Basics

NOW THAT YOU ARE MAGAZINE-PERFECT in your attire (great hat, temperature-savvy layers, and the best socks and boots in town), it's time to pack up and head out.

The Hiker's Dozen

I don't want to overwhelm you with so many requirements that you'll put off hitting the trail. But at the risk of having you close the book right here, I'm unveiling the venerable list known as the Hiker's Dozen. Common sense tells you that most of these items just won't be necessary on that 1-mile loop around the local park lake. However, one of the first rules of hiking is to *be prepared for anything.*

I honestly hope you will heed this list and assemble all of these aids in your pack. I keep mine ready to go except for the food and water that I add at the last minute. If you do the same, it takes only a few flicks of the wrist to remove anything you know you won't need at a particular destination; but if you don't keep all of this together in one place, as a matter of habit, then it will take a lot of time to round everything up when you do need it.

The best rule of thumb is that if you call what you are about to do a "hike" rather than a "walk," then please charge out the door with all 12 components in your pack. Enough said. Let's get on with this show!

❑ 1. WATER: Carry it in a hydration pack, such as those mentioned on pages 59 and 60, or in durable bottles such those made by Nalgene (my favorite), available in a wide choice of shapes, sizes, and colors.

❑ 2. MAP(S): Ideally, you should have a topographic map to show you the literal lay of the land, and also

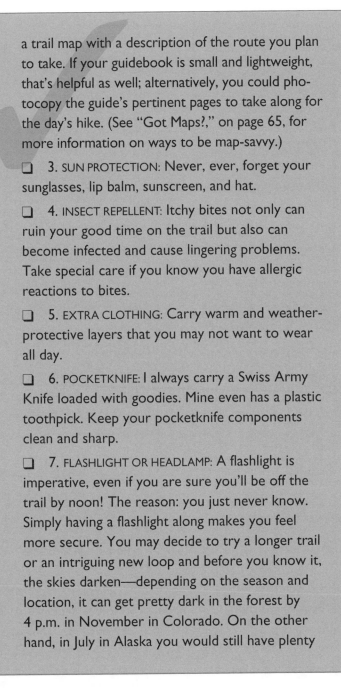

a trail map with a description of the route you plan
to take. If your guidebook is small and lightweight,
that's helpful as well; alternatively, you could pho-
tocopy the guide's pertinent pages to take along for
the day's hike. (See "Got Maps?," on page 65, for
more information on ways to be map-savvy.)

❑   3. SUN PROTECTION: Never, ever, forget your
sunglasses, lip balm, sunscreen, and hat.

❑   4. INSECT REPELLENT: Itchy bites not only can
ruin your good time on the trail but also can
become infected and cause lingering problems.
Take special care if you know you have allergic
reactions to bites.

❑   5. EXTRA CLOTHING: Carry warm and weather-
protective layers that you may not want to wear
all day.

❑   6. POCKETKNIFE: I always carry a Swiss Army
Knife loaded with goodies. Mine even has a plastic
toothpick. Keep your pocketknife components
clean and sharp.

❑   7. FLASHLIGHT OR HEADLAMP: A flashlight is
imperative, even if you are sure you'll be off the
trail by noon! The reason: you just never know.
Simply having a flashlight along makes you feel
more secure. You may decide to try a longer trail
or an intriguing new loop and before you know it,
the skies darken—depending on the season and
location, it can get pretty dark in the forest by
4 p.m. in November in Colorado. On the other
hand, in July in Alaska you would still have plenty

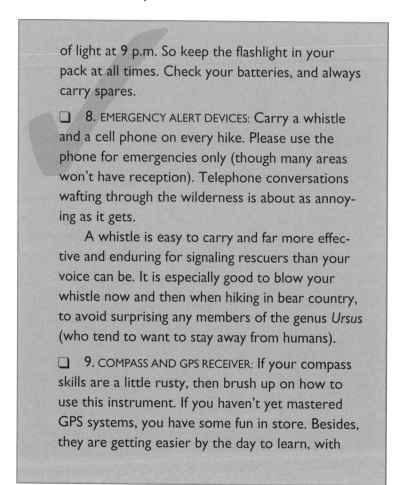

of light at 9 p.m. So keep the flashlight in your pack at all times. Check your batteries, and always carry spares.

❑ 8. EMERGENCY ALERT DEVICES: Carry a whistle and a cell phone on every hike. Please use the phone for emergencies only (though many areas won't have reception). Telephone conversations wafting through the wilderness is about as annoying as it gets.

A whistle is easy to carry and far more effective and enduring for signaling rescuers than your voice can be. It is especially good to blow your whistle now and then when hiking in bear country, to avoid surprising any members of the genus *Ursus* (who tend to want to stay away from humans).

❑ 9. COMPASS AND GPS RECEIVER: If your compass skills are a little rusty, then brush up on how to use this instrument. If you haven't yet mastered GPS systems, you have some fun in store. Besides, they are getting easier by the day to learn, with

DRINK UP

Number one on your list of hiking take-alongs must be water, but how much is enough? The American College of Sports Medicine (ACSM) recommends hydrating before exercise begins and then downing 8 to 10 ounces every 15 to 20 minutes while you are engaged in active pursuits. That may sound like a lot of water, but it is a good guideline. Obviously a slow-walking hiker doesn't need to replenish fluids as often

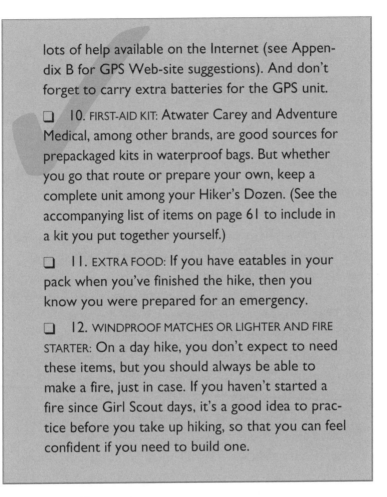

lots of help available on the Internet (see Appendix B for GPS Web-site suggestions). And don't forget to carry extra batteries for the GPS unit.

❏ 10. FIRST-AID KIT: Atwater Carey and Adventure Medical, among other brands, are good sources for prepackaged kits in waterproof bags. But whether you go that route or prepare your own, keep a complete unit among your Hiker's Dozen. (See the accompanying list of items on page 61 to include in a kit you put together yourself.)

❏ 11. EXTRA FOOD: If you have eatables in your pack when you've finished the hike, then you know you were prepared for an emergency.

❏ 12. WINDPROOF MATCHES OR LIGHTER AND FIRE STARTER: On a day hike, you don't expect to need these items, but you should always be able to make a fire, just in case. If you haven't started a fire since Girl Scout days, it's a good idea to practice before you take up hiking, so that you can feel confident if you need to build one.

as a racing mountain biker. Still, to avoid dehydration, you should always *err on the side of too much water.* You should never start to feel real thirst, because that's a sign that you're already dehydrating.

Using the above rule of thumb, you would want to have three to five 8-ounce bottles of water for every hour of hiking. A few years ago, Northern California–based CamelBak outfoxed water bottles with a nifty alternative called "hands-free hydration systems." Among many types of water-bladder backpacks available today, some are specifically designed for us—to fit the contours of our female bodies. In this line, CamelBak's Day Star style holds 70 ounces of water and is marketed as enough for 2 to 3 hours on a mountain bike or hiking trail. If you do the math, that works out to a minimum of 8 ounces every 20 minutes, or a maximum of 10 ounces every 15 minutes; that meshes with the previous ACSM guidelines for 2 to 3 hours of strenuous activity.

PACK *It* IN

Some hydration gear, such as CamelBak bags, have room for other hiking necessities—your extra layer of clothing, and items listed in "The Hiker's Dozen" (see page 56). Otherwise, you'll need an additional carrier that lets you swing your arms free. The hiking trail is no place for a fashion purse!

The first thing to consider when choosing a pack is whether you'll use it for a short day hike, overnight backpacking trips, or longer expeditions. Here, we will concentrate on day hikes. Part Seven, After Sundown, delves into more detail about overnight requirements.

Don't even consider fanny packs—they're not large enough to carry all that you will need. Look for a hip (lumbar) pack or a day pack (small backpack or rucksack). To me, a hip pack is the perfect choice for a day hike. It does just what it says: It wraps around your hips and fastens at the front of your body.

There are several levels of hip packs out there. (Mountainsmith makes my favorites.) In addition to standard, attached water-bottle holders, some have several compartments, plus hooks and straps. The ones with wide, padded straps can be adjusted to your body and are extremely comfortable.

Day packs are also good options. They are comfortable and have ample storage space. Just make sure you

First-aid Kit

A typical kit may contain more items than you think necessary, but these are just the basics, and they pack down into a small space:

Prescription and over-the-counter meds

❑ Personal medications

❑ Pain reliever, such as ibuprofen or acetaminophen

❑ Benadryl (or the generic equivalent, diphenhydramine) for allergic reactions

❑ Epinephrine in a prefilled syringe (usually by prescription only; if you hike with people who experience severe allergic reactions to bee stings and the like, make sure someone in your group carries this)

Injury and trauma ministrations

❑ Hydrogen peroxide, iodine, or any type of wound disinfectant (I like Band-Aid One-Step Protection Foam)

❑ Antibacterial and soothing creams, such as Neosporin or Aquaphor

❑ Bandages, including traditional Band-Aids, butterfly-closure bandages, and Ace bandages

❑ Gauze compress pads and a roll of gauze

❑ Moleskin

❑ Adhesive tape or medical tape

My Wish List

- ❏ Aluminum foil for wrapping lunch or snack leftovers and, in emergencies, collecting water and signaling for help
- ❏ Bandanna
- ❏ Carabiners
- ❏ Dark chocolate (look for bars with at least 60 percent real cocoa)
- ❏ Digital camera
- ❏ Disinfectant wipes or baby wipes
- ❏ Energy-drink mix (like Emergen-C)
- ❏ Extra batteries for electronics
- ❏ Garbage bag
- ❏ Hand warmers (air-activated)
- ❏ Journal
- ❏ Long pants or zip-on bottoms instead of extra pants (see "Go Shopping!" section)
- ❏ Mirror
- ❏ Panty liners and/or other feminine protection
- ❏ Permanent markers
- ❏ Plastic bags with zip closure
- ❏ Plastic grocery bags or doggie-poop pickup bags
- ❏ Snakebite kit
- ❏ Toilet paper
- ❏ Watch

Hike over to Part Seven: After Sundown

Starting on page 189, you will find information about the gear you'll need for overnight hiking and back-packing adventures. The Hiker's Dozen and first-aid kit remain the same whether you're on a day hike, a full-weekend outing, or a weeklong vacation.

don't overstuff the piece because it's so roomy. Believe me, you will not want any unnecessary weight on a hike— nor will your buddy want to hear you complain about it. Keep it simple and take only what you need to be pre-pared for the day.

As with hiking boots, you should investigate several packs before you buy one. I suggest going all out on this important decision:

• Ask the store clerk for something to put into the pack for a few minutes to sample how it feels with contents.

• Adjust the straps to accommodate your body.

• Walk around the store with the "loaded" pack.

• Make sure your water bottle would be quickly acces-sible on the *outside* of the pack.

• Take the pack on and off several times to see how that feels.

• Make the purchase, or keep looking!

The NICE-TO-HAVES

The more you hike, the more you will wish for certain things that you never thought you would miss on the trail. The chart on page 62 offers a starter list of some of my favorites. The watch and camera sound like no-brainers, but sometimes I do not want them with me.

Frankly, to me the journal is often a must-have, so it's nearly on my essentials list. But that is a personal proclivity. As you'll see from the special section "Journaling the Journey," I find that hiking and journaling combine like soul mates.

So, make your own lists for different seasons, and keep those reminders in your pack to check before you set out each time.

Got **Maps?**

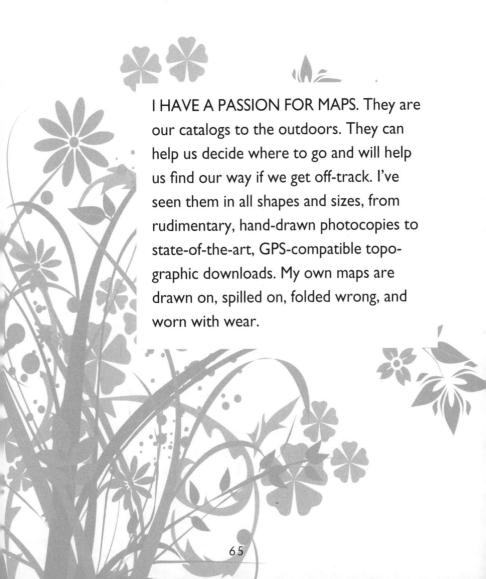

I HAVE A PASSION FOR MAPS. They are our catalogs to the outdoors. They can help us decide where to go and will help us find our way if we get off-track. I've seen them in all shapes and sizes, from rudimentary, hand-drawn photocopies to state-of-the-art, GPS-compatible topographic downloads. My own maps are drawn on, spilled on, folded wrong, and worn with wear.

That's because, for me, the study of maps is part of the fun of hiking. Hiking is a sensory experience (see "Sensual Stuff," page 101) that begins with the planning. Hundreds of books and Web resources allow you to read up on an area's plant- and wildlife. Use them to think about what your eyes will see, what your ears will hear, and what your nose will smell. But maps prepare you for the terrain itself—what your feet will touch.

When a trail is first laid out or hacked through, the originating agency, such as the U.S. Forest Service (USFS), takes great care to map the route. In the outdoor guidebooks that I author, I follow each trail with a GPS unit and then download the data into a topographical computer program. After the resulting map is manipulated and details are drawn in, it goes to my publisher, where an artist renders an appealing map for the book.

The keystone of all cartography in the United States is the topographical (topo) map inventory available from the U.S. Geological Survey (USGS). These maps are published in print format, and Topo USA and National Geographic produce digital versions of them for downloading. Once a map is on your computer, you can manipulate it onscreen, add your own notes, and print it out. However, I still prefer to lay the foldout, poster-sized topo map on the ground or floor and use my highlighter and various markers to map my route.

Many trails are mapped by several different entities, so you should be able to get your hands on at least two or three versions of maps for your chosen hike. The USFS, the National Park Service, the U.S. Bureau of Land Management, and state, county, and city park services typically put out recreational maps of the lands that they govern. You can also turn to outdoor guidebooks, Internet sites, and groups such as American Hiking Society (**www.americanhiking.org**) and **Trails.com.** Sometimes the most up-to-date maps are available at the trailheads—though don't ever count on that before you leave the house empty-handed. (Trailhead maps may be intended for you to borrow, or recycle, as signs may ask you to return them to the kiosk at the end of your hike. Instructions may also politely add, "Thank you for choosing this trail.")

MAP TALK

The USGS National Mapping Program uses a scale of 1:24,000 or 1:25,000 for our 50 states. (Translation: 1 inch on the map equals 24,000 on the ground, and it usually covers an area of 6 by 8 miles.)

Most maps organize the world into a tidy series of grids known as latitude and longitude, and the USGS is no exception. Latitude and longitude are expressed in units called degrees, minutes, and seconds, signifying distances north or south of the equator (for latitude) and east or west of a prime meridian that runs through Greenwich, England (for longitude). Tick marks on maps indicate latitude (on the left and right edges) or longitude (on top and bottom edges). If you draw a line connected to the opposite ticks, you create a grid.*

*FOR GPS USERS

In addition to the longitude/latitude grid system described above in "Map Talk," a newer methodology, Universal Transverse Mercator (UTM), is useful for GPS receivers. Map areas are divided into zones that are easier to pinpoint than latitude–longitude grids over Earth's curvature. USGS topo maps include grid tick marks and also recommends UTM coordinates for GPS systems.

So, in the USGS system, you will likely hear of 7.5-minute maps; that means each quadrangle of land or water area shown on the map is measured by its latitude and longitude degrees in units called minutes—with 7.5 longitude minutes and 7.5 latitude minutes. (An older series of USGS maps were based on a 15-minute quadrangle, but they are rare.)

COLOR CODE

The colors used on a USGS map are also full of meaning and are really fun to preview for hike-planning purposes:

• **Green** indicates heavy vegetation, usually in areas covered with forests, woodlands, or orchards.

• **White** denotes fields, meadows, rocky slopes, or other forms of open country.

• **Blue** means water. A large *patch* of blue is usually a pond or a lake. A blue *band* is a river, and a blue *line* is a stream. If the line is *broken,* the stream represented doesn't flow all year. Marshes and swamps are drawn with broken blue lines and tufts of grass. Names of all water features are given in italic type.

• **Black** indicates rail lines, bridges, boundaries, and the names of landmarks—anything that is the work of humans. Roads are shown as parallel black lines: solid for paved and improved gravel roads, broken for unimproved dirt roads. *A single black broken line is a hiking trail. (Very good to know!)* Black squares and rectangles are buildings: Solid black indicates inhabited structures, such as houses, schools, churches; outlined black symbolizes barns, sheds, and other outbuildings.

• **Thin brown lines** denote contours and surface features of an area—its hills, valleys, mountains, and plains. Each contour line relates to a specific elevation above sea level; that is, the elevation remains the same at all points along any one contour line. The closer together the lines, the steeper the terrain. Where the lines are far apart, the slope of the ground is gentle. This is important information when you are deciding on a hike.

DO Maps LIE?

You should generally assume that all maps are accurate, but if your senses tell you that a map is wrong, you may just be right. Maps are more accurate than ever due to satellite technology, but this science has also hindered efforts to complete the lengthy and laborious process called "ground-truthing," whereby topographers set out onto the land and map it on foot. (Back to the days of Lewis and Clark!) *So always take a peek at your map's legend to see when it was created. An outdated map could get you into trouble, depending on the remoteness of your destination. Even in more urban locations, the roadways may have changed due to some fancy overpass going in.*

The SUN and the STARS

A huge component of reading maps and always knowing where you are is orientation. And to really orient yourself, you must hone your sense of direction. Beyond map reading, you will want to renew your relationship with the sun and the stars. Don't be shy if you need a refresher. I know many people who are intelligent and sophisticated, but they can easily get turned around, even in urban environments loaded with street signs, because they don't stop to think about basic direction. So here goes:

Remember that the sun can always help you stay oriented. In the morning, it rises to the east, and in the evening it sets to the west. To locate approximate north, turn your right shoulder toward the early morning sun and you will be facing north.

In the late afternoon, the sun is in the west. Turn your left shoulder toward the sun and you will be facing approximate north. Either time, when you are facing north, east is to your right, west is to your left and south is behind you. Where I live, the mountains are to the west, so they always serve as a wonderful orientation tool when I leave the house.

The classic survival skill down through the ages has been, and continues to be, knowing how to find the North Star or, if your prefer the lyrical Latin name as I do, Polaris. On a clear night, Polaris will anchor the north for you. This star's light is not particularly bright, but the star forms the tip of the Little Dipper's handle. So that's where you start. The nearby Big Dipper is fairly easy for most people to readily discern, so look for the two pointer stars on the outer edge of the Big Dipper's bowl. Once you have sights on those two pointer stars, draw an imaginary line between them, straight to the star at the tip of the Little Dipper. There you are: Polaris. The good news, especially for the ancient explorers, is that Polaris is always in the same relative position in the sky when viewed from the Northern Hemisphere.

COMPASS 101

The compass determines direction with a steel needle attracted by the magnetism of the earth. When at rest, the needle points to the north end of this giant magnet. The magnetic North Pole of the earth is considered true north and is different from the geographic north indicated on most maps. The numbers on a compass are called degrees or bearings. A compass has 360 degrees, that is, 90 degrees is the same as east.

Here's a refresher on basic terms you'll need to know when working with a compass:

• **Compass housing** encloses the needle.

• A **magnetized needle** moves inside the compass housing and always points north when at rest.

• **Degree readings** are 360 directions you can travel from any point.

• The **orienting arrow** is the set of parallel lines inside the housing.

• **Cardinal points** are north, south, east, and west.

• **Intercardinal (ordinal)** points are northeast, northwest, southwest, and southeast—the four positions between the cardinal points.

• The **direction-of-travel arrow** points in the direction to go after the compass is set.

• The **transparent base** shows the direction-of-travel arrow and a scale of millimeters and inches for computing distance on a map.

When you want to use the compass to follow direction in relation to a map, first orient the map to north by turning the map, with the compass on it, until the magnetic needle rests over the orienting arrow, pointing to north.

If you want to go from point A to point B, place the edge of the plastic base of the compass along the line of travel from A to B, with the direction-of-travel arrow pointing toward B. Turn the compass housing until the orienting arrow points north, parallel with the vertical line on the map. The degree reading for point B lies along the direction-of-travel arrow. To calculate distance, first measure the distance from point A to point B with the millimeter rule on the plastic base of the compass. Then check the map scale in the margin to convert measurement to meters (feet) or kilometers (miles) for the distance between A and B.

Declination is the angle between the direction the compass needle points (magnetic north) and the geographic or true North Pole of the earth. Geographic or true north and magnetic north are not the same place. It is important to ascertain the local declination because your intended course will not be correct if you depend on a compass direction taken from a map without considering the declination. The declination can usually be found in the margin or legend of a map.

Another solution is to use a GPS unit of a compass that can be adjusted so that its readings are aligned with true north rather than magnetic north. Once the adjustment has been made, the compass uses as its reference any true-north map lines.

Phew! Nothing is simpler, in practice, than using a map or a compass and then using a map and a compass together. However, nothing is more difficult to describe, unless it is shown in person, on the trail. Be assured that once you do get the hang of it, you'll be fine. A great way to practice is to use a map of your neighborhood and a compass and take a walk around the block practicing these navigation skills.

Pack *a* **Picnic**

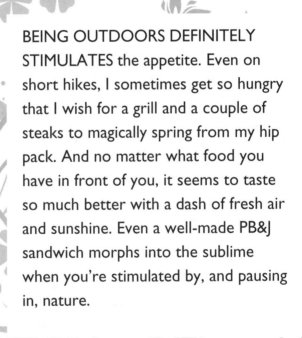

BEING OUTDOORS DEFINITELY STIMULATES the appetite. Even on short hikes, I sometimes get so hungry that I wish for a grill and a couple of steaks to magically spring from my hip pack. And no matter what food you have in front of you, it seems to taste so much better with a dash of fresh air and sunshine. Even a well-made PB&J sandwich morphs into the sublime when you're stimulated by, and pausing in, nature.

On a recent hike with a friend, we compared lunches and sadly realized that we had scraped the bare bones of our pantries. I began to recite a menu that would have been more appropriate for our alfresco setting: brie on crusty bread, fresh tomatoes with basil leaves, and moist chocolate brownies. It made me commit to putting a little more thought into my hiking fare. After all, food is a necessary element in the outdoors for safety and survival, and not being hungry is essential to the success of the experience.

You are limited in food choices, somewhat, by the space available in your pack. And despite my fantasies, we all should also probably restrict ourselves to foods that require no grills and no cooking on the trail. This isn't camping after all—it's day hiking. (Move on to Part Seven, After Sundown, if you pine for a campfire dinner followed by a sleeping tent.)

Because you will be carrying your meal and snacks in your pack, you should build your menu around simple, whole foods (fruits, vegetables, grains, nuts, cured cold cuts) that travel well and that can *safely* withstand being out of the refrigerator for the time between home and trail break. Foods you can enjoy without using utensils make packing easier, and there's less cleanup. Also take heed that your food needs to be protected from your body heat and from your bounce along the trail while you hike.

Hard cheeses, hearty breads, small packages of nuts, and fruits such as apples and oranges all hold up well without a lot of insulation. For sandwiches and more delicate items, such as cherry tomatoes or crackers, use lightweight metal or plastic containers that hold food snugly but don't smoosh it. Nothing is worse than being ravenous on the trail and pulling a poorly wrapped, mayonnaise-soggy sandwich from the pack. Well, maybe the only thing worse is how your pack smells until you can get it wiped down and aired out. At least such mistakes are so memorable that they guarantee better planning henceforth.

BEWARE *of* UNDEREATING!

Hiking requires a lot of energy and burns calories. (Yeah!) So plan your trail meals and snacks around nourishment and extra energy. An energy bar or some form of GORP (Good Old Raisins and Peanuts) can give you a healthful boost between meals, especially if you are out longer that you anticipated. Your own favorite indulgence is a must—mine is dark chocolate. It serves many purposes: energy source, mood enhancer, and friend maker. (Have I really mentioned chocolate six times already in this book?)

Now is not the time to skimp on food or nutrients—even if you are on a diet to lose weight. In fact, if you are using hiking as a weight-management tool, you must remember to eat right. Managing your blood sugar while exercising helps reduce cravings, curbs binge eating, and keeps you from crashing due to low blood sugar. You must keep your insulin levels low and steady so your body can use your fat stores as fuel.

For weight reduction, I do suggest going easy on the sweets while hiking. (And I promise to stop mentioning chocolate.) Also check food labels to minimize your consumption of hidden sweeteners, such as honey and high-fructose corn syrup. Aim to consume at least 25 percent of your day's calorie allotment during your morning meal, and enjoy a hearty breakfast before the hike. Whole-grain oatmeal with blackberries or hard-boiled eggs and slices of rye bread make good morning choices that won't spike your blood sugar.

In planning your picnic, do not mix fats and simple carbohydrates. Fats consumed with insulin-raising foods are more likely to be stored as fat. When eating an avocado, for instance, combine it with whole-grain bread rather than the

refined carbs of white bread. Whatever you do, *don't under-
eat on the trail,* especially at midday. That can backfire. Your
small midday meal may satisfy you temporarily, but you will
crave calories later.

Dieting or not, any hiker will want to go lightly on products made from white flour or white rice; they can affect
your blood sugar. You don't have to avoid such foods if you
enjoy them, but consider keeping the portions small and,
again, focusing on whole grains and other energy-producing
sustenance.

FOOD SAFETY

I follow the two-hour rule for all perishables that would
otherwise be in the fridge: consume them within two hours
of prep. The danger of food poisoning rises after that. If you
are carrying something that should remain cold, put it into an
insulated bag with a freezer gel. (Do you know that thanks
to modern technology, you can actually haul a pint of Ben
& Jerry's on the trail these days and keep it rock-hard? Yes.
Granite Gear's zippered one-pint Air Cooler is suspiciously
perfect for, well, some Cherry Garcia . . . or maybe some
Chunky Monkey. In one mountaineering store, they promote
it for just that task.)

Just because you'll be hiking doesn't mean you can't add
something warm to your meal plan. Small thermoses are
great for soup on the trail, and the thermos lid serves triples
as bowl and "sipper," so you don't even need a spoon.

If you want something fancier than finger foods, don't
forget to pack the utensils you need. You can of course use
your pocketknife as a picnic accoutrement. However, the
French company Opinel is justifiably known for its classic
(and economically priced) folding picnic knife; the handmade
piece lasts for decades of outdoor fares.

Whatever you do, your outdoor gourmandizing should *not* require complex preparations. That would impinge on time for your trail wanderlust! Focus on one or two main courses, such as a thick sandwich and some crudités, or hearty soup and crackers. Robust bread, a good cheese, and fresh fruit will round it into a spectacular meal—especially when surrounded by the appetite booster of nature. On your limited-time days, do not stint on your hike because your cupboard is bare. Have a *walk-out* picnic. This is when you *walk out* of a grocery store, deli, or sandwich shop with your ready-made repast and head for the trailhead.

Make new friends, but keep the old. One is silver, and the other gold.

—*Classic Girl Scout camp song*

PART THREE

A WORD *about* TRAIL MATES

The **Buddy** *System*

HIKING WITH A FRIEND is like having a built-in security system, potential medic, and rescuer right by your side. So you want to pick your companions wisely, because they could save your life. The buddy system is about the best insurance policy you can have on the trail. Imagine how difficult it would be to splint your own broken ankle, versus having your friend help you; or how impossible it would be to get yourself out of a deep ravine or crevice if you were alone. Plus, how nice to have someone to share that beautiful view, or gossip with over your lunch break.

One Boy Scout leader told me that he teaches troop members to hike with a minimum of four people. In case of anyone's injury, that allows someone to stay with the victim and two people to hike out for help.

Don't be another Aron Ralston: I think everyone who used to think nothing of hiking alone, especially in familiar areas, got a wake-up call back in 2003. That's when a smart, experienced mountain climber named Aron Ralston was hiking alone in a Utah canyon, and a boulder fell and pinned his right arm. After five days of being trapped, he broke the bones in his own arm in order to cut through the muscle and tissue with a pocketknife and free himself. Although he was extremely resourceful, if he had been hiking with a companion, this story would probably have had a different outcome. (Ralston, who has gone on to hike more mountains, tells this terrifying story in his book, *Between a Rock and a Hard Place,* and you can see his original recounting with Tom Brokaw at YouTube; go to **www.youtube.com** and search for "Aron Ralston describes the amputation.")

Finding partners: I know all too well that it may be difficult to draft hiking partners, for a lot of reasons. Getting two or more schedules to sync is culprit number one. So try to work with your friends' hobbies and interests in order to lure them to the trails. Bird-watching, caving, and photography are great ploys to entice people out with you—if those are their particular passions.

Many universities, gyms, and local parks and recreation departments post or publish hiking activities, and hiking groups are springing up across the country. For just a taste of this trend, log on to American Hiking Society's site, at **www .americanhiking.org;** click on "Partners," then "View our Alliance members." You'll find a pull-down menu with dozens of clubs and organizations state by state. For example, the site

shows 18 different groups of interest to me for hiking partners and trail volunteerism all over my own state of Colorado. There is the Friends of Dinosaur Ridge, in Morrison; the
Headwaters Trails Alliance, in Granby; Trails 2000, in Denver;
and the Colorado Mountain Club, in Golden, just to give you
an idea of the types of listings. Altogether, this is an impressive source of opportunities for me—and you—to join others
who not only love hiking but who also are helping to keep
each state's natural environment walkable.

But maybe you don't want to get involved with a formal
group. Maybe you want to keep it more neighborly. So . . .
how about posting a note at your local outdoor-gear store
or online? If you find yourself with "takers," be sure your
numbers are great enough that you don't put yourself in a
potentially dangerous situation. One stranger signing up for
the "group" and the two of you heading out for a day together
in the forest is not what I had in mind with this suggestion!

The above cautionary note does, however, bring up
another friend's story. It falls into the "What was I thinking?" category: Years ago, against her better judgment, she
accepted an invitation for a hike in California's Sierra Nevada
foothills with a man she had met briefly at a small gathering.
As she headed out the door to join him for the hike, she
looked around for some weapon she might take. That turned
out to be a handful of sharpened yellow pencils, which she
stuck into her waist pack. Fortunately, she not only lived to
laugh about this story but also ended up dating the fellow
for quite a few months before she decided he was no hiking
partner for life.

The **More** the Merrier?

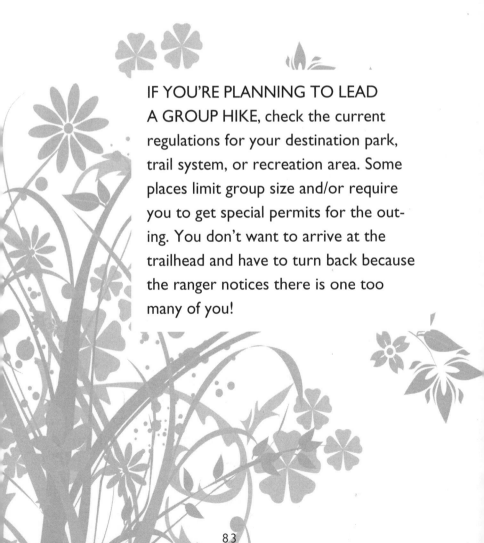

IF YOU'RE PLANNING TO LEAD A GROUP HIKE, check the current regulations for your destination park, trail system, or recreation area. Some places limit group size and/or require you to get special permits for the outing. You don't want to arrive at the trailhead and have to turn back because the ranger notices there is one too many of you!

Group Protocol

On the trail, these tips practically guarantee a successful group venture:

❏ Designate "lead" and "back" hikers to assure no one gets lost, but beware of separating them too far apart, because the people in between can still take wrong turns.

❏ Stay together, and *never* split up a group. "Separated group syndrome" is a common search-and-rescue scenario.

❏ From the outset, share responsibilities (such as watching out for each other) and encourage questions.

❏ Check in with each person often enough to be sure everyone is OK.

Before the hiking day arrives, get some gauge of each participant's previous outdoor experience. This is especially smart if you are setting out for a day-long expedition or heading for challenging countryside. Let each person know exactly what the trip entails in terms of mileage and terrain.

Be sure to also describe anticipated payoffs, such as fall color, waterfalls, or bird migrations. Provide the hikers with a current trail map and a checklist of the gear they will need to have in their packs. (See "The Hiker's Dozen," on page 56.) I recommend scheduling "shakedown hikes," or a series of increasingly arduous practice runs before ambitious trips. This way, the group will know that you mean business about

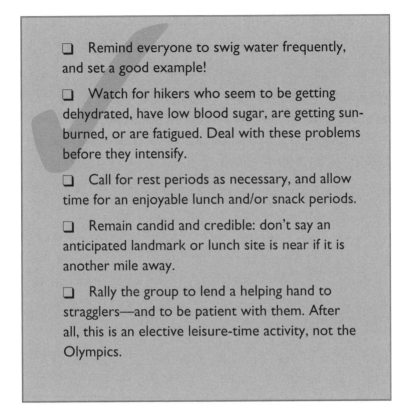

❑   Remind everyone to swig water frequently, and set a good example!

❑   Watch for hikers who seem to be getting dehydrated, have low blood sugar, are getting sunburned, or are fatigued. Deal with these problems before they intensify.

❑   Call for rest periods as necessary, and allow time for an enjoyable lunch and/or snack periods.

❑   Remain candid and credible: don't say an anticipated landmark or lunch site is near if it is another mile away.

❑   Rally the group to lend a helping hand to stragglers—and to be patient with them. After all, this is an elective leisure-time activity, not the Olympics.

being prepared for the Big Day—and that you care enough about them and about the feat that lies ahead that you want everyone to be ready and fired up to enjoy it.

On the day of the hike, quietly determine that each hiker has what she will need to be comfortable—and safe. Depending on how generous you feel, and how much you want to carry in your own pack, you can have extra gear on hand. But if someone shows up wearing flip-flops, with nothing but a camera and an 8-ounce bottle of water for a rugged 10-mile hike, it's perfectly reasonable to ask her to join you at another time. (Remember, it is often the person who is most careless about preparation who becomes the loudest complainer when she feels some discomfort, so you owe it to the group to stick to your guns!) But handle this quietly and out of earshot of the other participants.

If indeed you find yourself in a situation where you need outside help, you have many options. First, try to stay with your hiking party and come up with a plan together. If some-one in the group is injured, send preferably two hikers to get help while the others remain with the injured party.

If you are hiking with only one other person, flag down other hikers if you hear or see them nearby and ask for their help—which is almost always forthcoming. Be sure that those who go for help remember where the injured party is! If you are going for help and have a GPS, note the coordinates. Without a GPS, use a little creativity and leave or memorize natural visual markers (rocks, logs, trees) to alert you and rescuers of the way back when you return.

For more information about emergency situations—such as if you are in a position where no one can get help, espe-cially if you have only one hiking companion—see Part Six, Mama Said There'd Be Days Like This!, on page 157.

Diverse Companions, Different Abilities

I HAVE FRIENDS AND ACQUAIN-
TANCES who have conditions that may
hinder them from fully participating in
some sports. If you have discounted
hiking or nature walking as a possibil-
ity for those friends, I think you will be
happy to know you have more options.
Across the United States, many walking paths can accommodate a sturdy
wheelchair, for example. Such courses
may be paved or smooth natural
surfaces, such as hard-packed dirt.

Many individuals with limitations in one sense have heightened abilities in other senses. They might enjoy nature in some ways more than the average person with perfect sight, hearing, or mobility. For example, many individuals with visual impairments have extremely keen senses of hearing and/or smell. Take a walk on an appropriate trail with such a friend, and you might develop a new awareness of the sound of insects or the fragrance of a blossom—things you took for granted in the past.

Day camps, overnight camps, and programs through local agencies also conduct special needs hikes. There are sport camps for the blind and visually impaired; for people with moderate mental challenges; for sensory impairments; for learning disabilities; for attention-deficit/hyperactivity disorder; for people with diabetes or asthma. Whether they require an attendant, are moderately independent, or are totally independent, these individuals generally gain skills, self-esteem, confidence, and fitness when given opportunities for outdoor exposure and activity.

Woman's
Best *Friend*

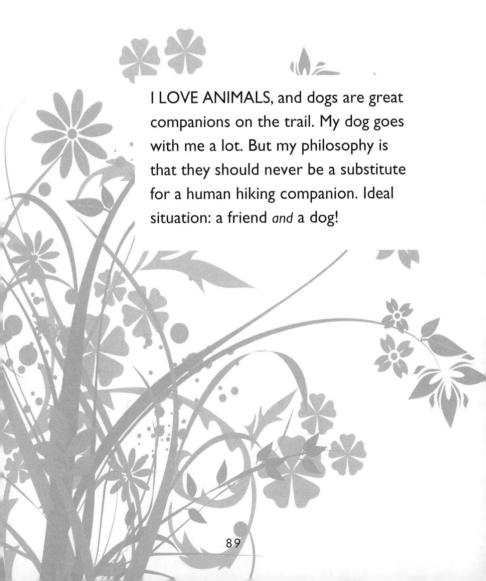

I LOVE ANIMALS, and dogs are great companions on the trail. My dog goes with me a lot. But my philosophy is that they should never be a substitute for a human hiking companion. Ideal situation: a friend *and* a dog!

Dogs on trails can cause problems, so I offer some guidelines for taking your hound into the wild.

Leashing Roverina is the only way to absolutely prevent her from chasing wildlife and other trail users. A six-foot leash allows enough room for her to enjoy the trail without getting tangled in underbrush or other hikers. And, by the way, horses have the right-of-way around dogs, but the two species often alarm each other, so here again: keep a good hold on that leash.

Leashing dogs also keeps them from getting lost, and protects them from wildlife attacks because they aren't running loose and provoking other creatures. Nothing is worse than taking a dog to the veterinarian to pull out the porcupine quills lodged in its sinuses.

Leashing also gives you control over your dog drinking from streams and other water sources they seem to want to run to. "Found" water and even beautiful springs can harbor harmful bacteria, such as the widely dreaded *Giardia intestinalis*. This one-celled parasite is a threat to dogs as well as to humans. *Always* pack fresh water for your dog for the trail. To avoid dehydration, dogs require just as much water in ratio to their body weight as humans. If you notice sunken eyes, dry mouth, and lethargy, your dog desperately needs water—NOW!

A healthy dog should be able to carry up to a third of its weight in a special pack, as my dog does when we hike together. (Dog packs, along with collapsible water bowls, are available at outdoor and pet stores.) Just like you, your dog must be in adequately good physical shape before undertaking a hike. Start off small, then work up to longer hikes. Make sure that your dog is protected with up-to-date vaccinations for rabies, bordatella, and heartworms, and that his or her medications are current. If you are hiking in an area with

ticks that can cause Lyme disease, ask your vet about vaccinations for that protection.

Remember that dogs can get hurt on the trail just like
you. My dog has had the hair between her paws become
encrusted with ice. So try to protect their paws with dog
booties when the trails are cold and icy. (Sled-dog mushers,
such as those in Alaska's annual Iditarod Race, are required
to provide booties for their animals.)

If you're taking your dog on the trail, always prepare for
accidents. Keep your pet in mind when packing antibiotic
cream and self-sticking bandage tape in your first-aid kit.
After a hike, carefully check your dog (and yourself) for ticks
and burrs.

And, for fun, say the word *hike* to your dog each time
you're going to follow up immediately with that activity.
Pretty soon, he or she will be pawing the trail maps with you.

"I'm the walkingest girl around. I like to work at it—really get my heart pounding."

—*Amy Yasbeck, actress*

PART FOUR

HIT the TRAIL

Fit *Hiking*

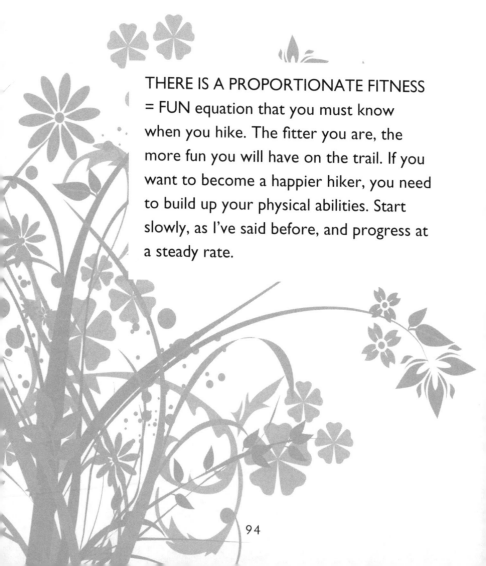

THERE IS A PROPORTIONATE FITNESS
= FUN equation that you must know
when you hike. The fitter you are, the
more fun you will have on the trail. If you
want to become a happier hiker, you need
to build up your physical abilities. Start
slowly, as I've said before, and progress at
a steady rate.

Even if you are accomplished in other sports, I predict you will find that hiking works your body in ways you may not be used to. It's an entirely different ball game. Over the years, a variety of people have joined me on the trail, with every level of fitness you can imagine. But I'd say most of them participate in other sports and are in great shape—my sister, for example. She runs, does yoga and Pilates, spins, plays volleyball, and lives right on the beach.

But I recall the time we got to the trailhead for an 8-mile hike and she said we should be up and back in less than two hours. I told her we were looking at a long day, since it was a hard hike. She couldn't comprehend that, because 8 miles on the paved path that runs by her house would take her less than 90 minutes. With the terrain we traveled, it took us four hours. (No, I didn't say "told you so.")

Finesse in other sports can skew perspective about the rigors of hiking over challenging terrain. If friends haven't hiked in a couple of weeks or months, I can always sense their labored breathing and am sensitive to the need for rest times. *Note:* Never push a hiking partner to walk faster or longer than she wants. Sometimes, the faster person needs to slow down!

I, too, go through periods where I may average four hikes a week and then go for weeks with no exercise. It can be an uphill battle, literally. But there are some things you can do to get into better shape for hiking, as well as to *stay* in shape for this sport. Here's my formula:

Start with short (1- to 3-mile) hikes a couple of times a week. Steadily increase the length of the walk until you are comfortable doing an easy 8-mile hike. Next, bump up the difficulty of your hike, while you try to maintain 8 trail miles a week. Here's a case where the whole (8 miles) is greater than the sum of its parts: That's because you can break that distance into two or three hikes over the week, and do them in any combination of moderate and difficult trails. (What's the best way to track hiking mileage, you ask? Personally, I total mileage on my GPS, but before I got that, I relied on my pedometer. See "Pedometers," on page 99).

If you follow the above prescription, you will begin to combine intensity with endurance. Continue to increase the distance and difficulty until you are ready to tackle all-day hikes and can train on more challenging terrain. You may go on to become interested in backpacking, for overnight adventures on longer hiking trips (see Part Seven, After Sundown). But please know that there is a huge difference between hiking on single days and hiking on multiple, consecutive days. The wear and tear on—and rewards to—your body are much greater, so you need to condition yourself for true backpacking, which is more than carrying a day pack or lumbar pack for a few hours.

Between writing projects and in the months before hiking season begins, a personal trainer helps me maintain my fitness and toughen up for the season. I strive for a healthy combination of rest, strength training, cardio, endurance, and cross-training. It's possible to work your whole system in less than an hour in the gym. If time is tight before your first hike in a while—or ever—don't panic. The key is to start slowly on any program. Unlike cramming for a college exam, we can't stay up all night studying our bodies into shape for a big hike at 8 a.m.

Since hiking trails are rarely flat, it is better to strength-train your muscles to propel you up and down the trail. You'll improve balance and agility at the same time. I've seen plenty of pre-season fitness programs, and the following is an intensive yet worthwhile weekly schedule that works for me. It requires time and commitment. But I believe you are reading this book because you *want* to make fitness more a part of your life.

Kim's Pre-season Fitness Training	
MONDAY	Your day of rest. It's as simple as that.
TUESDAY & THURSDAY	This is a strength-training day best completed in a gym. Building muscle is a keystone to any fitness program. Your best bet here is to get the help of a trainer to hold you accountable to your goals and help you complete the rest of your program.
WEDNESDAY & FRIDAY	Cardio days. Run, walk, sprint, but whatever you do, try to focus on interval training. That means you'll be alternating between slow and fast speed, between intensity and recovery motions. For example: power walk using your arms and legs, as fast as you can, for a few minutes; then walk slowly for twice as long; then switch the procedure and do the fast walk for twice as long as the slow walk. Interval training will increase your speed on the trail, burn more fat, and make you better able to cover more ground.
SATURDAY	Endurance hike. Take a long walk on varied terrain. If you are working toward a long-distance trek or an all-day hike, pack some of the gear you will need on that trip and carry it as part of your training. Keep increasing the gear on each walk until you have mastered the weight and stamina needed for the planned adventure.
SUNDAY	Pick a sport and have fun with it today: yoga, mountain biking, spinning, running, Pilates, you name it.

HIKING *for* TOTAL MIND–BODY *Fitness*

We all know that a walk around the block can clear your head and allow you to **reduce stress,** so why not a hike? The first thing to do is find an easy, quiet place, preferably a trail around a lake or in the woods or park, as opposed to a trail near a road. Keep your pace comfortable and your stride short. Focus on your breathing with deep inhales. With each exhale, imagine releasing tightness throughout your body. Spend several full, deep breaths on each part, one by one. Many people call this "meditation hiking." Starting from the top, make this journey:

Head	Fingers	*Mula bandha* area
Hair	Chest	(see page 8)
Ears	Upper back	Upper thighs
Neck	(around your	Knees
Shoulders	"wings")	Calves
Upper arms	Diaphragm	Ankles
Elbows	Belly	Feet
Forearms	Lower Back	Toes
Wrists	Buttocks or	
Hands	"glutes"	

If you want to hike for **better posture,** that's a worthy goal. All of the hiking in the world won't do you any good if you are jostling your spine, tweaking your knees, or overtaxing your muscles. If you get in the habit of practicing proper posture and alignment, you will reduce wear and tear on your bones, joints, and ligaments, and help your body rediscover its inherent alignment. Again, find an easy trail where you can focus on the task at hand. Start by lifting your crown and don't jut your head or chin; that can throw your neck

Pedometers

Pronounced "peh-DOM-eeter, a pedometer tracks your number of steps, translates that tally into distances you travel, and also counts the calories you've burned. (*Ped-* is short for "pedestrian," and *-meter* denotes measure.) A good one is not hard to find, and it doesn't have to be expensive. Among the best sellers at Amazon.com, prices ranged from $2.95 to $189. Like GPS machines, they come in many shapes and sizes. Some clip onto your clothes, some are like watches, and some, like mine, are built into a GPS. Some features to look for:

• Large, easy-to-read display with a clock

• Seven-day history, for review and comparison of a week's worth of exercise

• Dual-sensor technology to enable you to carry the machine in a holster, pocket, or a bag—it doesn't have to be in your hand.

and spine out of alignment. Next, engage your core, don't clench your glutes, and finally, shorten your stride.

Hiking for **inspiration** can set the stage for major mental breakthroughs. Here are some guidelines for using your hike to get out of a rut and lure your creativity into the open:

• Choose a hiking destination where you can expect no or minimal distraction. Once you are there, do some warm-up walking, then set a comfortable pace.

• Visualize the issue or idea you need clarity on. Your mind will inevitably wander, so let it. Then guide your thoughts back. This play between conscious and unconscious thinking stimulates your brain and opens you up to inspiration.

• Don't think about time; the average amount of time people (yours truly included) require to have a burst of creativity in this kind of conducive situation is about 15 minutes, or 1 mile of easy hiking. With that equation, you may have four great ideas in one hour!

Sensual *Stuff*

ON A RECENT HIKE, my companions and I passed a group of folks watching birds. We must have tossed up a bunch of dust, because one guy reminded us to slow down or we would never see anything. On the way back, the same cluster didn't look as if they had accomplished any mileage. You could, however, tell that they were actually seeing things and really appreciating every minute of their adventure. This was a real eye-opener for me. Especially when I am on a deadline, and the hike is part of a work or writing project, I definitely forget to slow down and look around.

Another outdoorswoman that I follow once said that she'd rather walk to the top of a mountain than drive there. She says that the same applies to getting outdoors in general: the world looks different at 2 miles an hour; spring comes one flower at a time; the wind cools the skin and a snowflake stings the tongue. . . . It's a way to reconnect with a simpler world and with ourselves.

The senses are our detectives in the natural world. They help us to tune in to our brains, perceive better, and remember more. When we use all of our senses, we can focus on the nature around us and become more aware of the things we usually pass by without noticing. Try a few of the following exercises on your next hike, and use them constantly to increase your awareness.

LOOK, Listen, TOUCH, Smell, TASTE, Intuit, and DESCRIBE

There are, of course, our textbook *five* senses. But I want to lead you on a hike using what I call our *seven* senses.

First, let's focus our **sight.** Take something small and circular that you can use to *limit your area of observance.* A rubber band will do, or a piece of string tied to make a circle. Put it on the ground and examine carefully what you find within the circle. Bring a small magnifying glass on one of your hikes and use that for a close-up of anything that strikes your fancy—rocks, leaves, bugs—and note all the shapes and colors of the object that you won't see with the proverbial naked eye.

In her book *Bird by Bird: Some Instructions on Writing and Life,* best-selling author Anne Lamott offers a similar exercise to help writers prime their creativity. She suggests buying one of those miniature frames from an art-supply

or hobby store, removing the backing, and then holding
the frame up to focus on whatever you aim it toward: the
corner of a chair, the eye of your dog, the picture of your
baby. Whatever. Then write about what you see through
that small frame. You can do that on the trail as well, and
you don't have to invest in a little frame. Just bring along a
small cardboard tube (like from a toilet paper roll). What
do you see when you hold it up and peer through it? Really
study it and think about it.

Lie on your back and watch the movement of the clouds
as they drift by. Lie on your stomach and look down. Crawl
on the ground and watch things from an animal's point of
view. Look for movement and evidence of change. Take a
picture with your eyes. Look at a scene and try to remember
everything about it. Look at a pebble, a pinecone, a bird, and
try to remember everything about it. Look for colors, patterns, textures, curves, and lines. Look for shapes in nature:
squares, circles, triangles.

Use your little magnifying glass, binoculars held back-
wards, or a water drop to zoom in on the details of something small. Count the rings on a tree stump. Look under a
rock, in a cave, in the mud or snow. Look up, look down,
look all around.

Our next sense is **hearing,** or listening. To practice, sit
blindfolded or lie down, close your eyes, and pay attention to
the different sounds, and at different times of day: tall grass
rustling, baby birds, a coyote. Listen for sounds nearby or
far away: a thunderstorm, an ant pulling a dried leaf, a train
whistle.

Are there sounds you like and sounds you dislike? A
tweety bird versus a bulldozer? Do you hear occasional
sounds and constant sounds, such as one dog barking or
a chorus of frogs?

Listen for sounds that change your emotions—sounds that make you angry, sad, happy, or scared. Do you hear noises from living things and sounds from machines? Hike with a small digital recorder to hang on to your favorite sounds. Follow a sound to find out what makes it. Decide which musical instruments produce sounds similar to those found in nature. Find examples and listen to music meant to evoke feelings of the out-of-doors. Start a collection of songs that have relevance to the outdoors, and play them at home.

To explore your sense of **touch,** examine the texture of bark, leaves, soil, feathers, pebbles, and something as simple as your hiking boot. Bring your hiking buddy into the exercise and have him or her hold something for you in a paper bag. (Definitely pick a partner you can trust for this—no practical jokers allowed!) Reach in and describe what you are feeling without looking at it. Feel with your fingers, the back of one hand, both hands together.

How do you feel in the shade? How do you feel in the sunlight? How many ways can you feel the wind? Can you find things that the wind has changed?

Our next sense is that of **smell.** Take a breath and deeply inhale the outdoors that's all around you. Sniff the flowers, of course. But also take a good whiff of leaves, ferns, bugs, soil, mud, and water. Some of my favorite tree barks and tree sap smell like butterscotch. Follow a scent; where does it lead? What does rain smell like? How does your destination smell after a storm or a small rain shower? What does the forest smell like when it's been heated up on a toasty summer day? Pinch a leaf, stem, or root, and then smell it.

A fifth sense, **taste,** does not get such an active workout in nature, other than the perception that anything we eat on a hike seems to activate our taste buds geometrically. While that definitely is worth noting, let's move on to our sixth sense,

intuition. Think about the understanding that often comes our way as we walk in nature. It goes back to the theme I've woven throughout this book, which is that the outdoor world delivers us to a state of clarity and self-knowledge. When we "attune to nature," as they say, we seem to plumb deeper into our own subconscious state of clairvoyance. As we hike along, we will know something to be true, or not true, right or not right, while all the facts in the world hadn't convinced us in the course of our busy indoor lives.

Here is where I take liberties and add a seventh sense: our ability to **describe.** I think of it as a sense because it is the union of what we have seen, heard, touched, smelled, tasted, and intuited. That is what you do when you talk to friends, family, or coworkers, or write in your journal.

An exercise for this is to describe how you feel when you think of your favorite place on a hike. Contemplate objects to use as benchmarks of size. Is what you are recounting as small as a dime? About the size of your palm? As big as a car? Use analogies to tell or show where things are.

If you are with a group, relay something that is unnoticed by anyone but yourself. A common way to do this is to imagine your area as the face of a clock. "If you're standing at the lookout, facing the valley, what I saw was at 11 o'clock," for example. (This is especially good for sighting and citing wildlife in the sky, up the trees, and on the ground.)

We can tap into our descriptive sense not only through speech, but also by drawing or painting what we see. You don't have to be a showcase-gallery artist to sketch a plant or flower from memory. Try that, then go outside or on a hike and take a good look at the plant or flower you had rendered. Look at it in its natural surroundings. Do a second drawing while looking at the plant, then compare the two results.

NIGHT LIGHTS

Camping out overnight is not the only way to enjoy the sensual vitality of nature at dusk, twilight, or by moon and starlight. (If you are interested in overnight backpacking, see Part Seven, After Sundown, on page 189.)

Many eco-resorts and lodges offer night hikes, and many are led by naturalists. You can safely assemble your own starlight safari if you have a well-known destination, you are with friends or family, and everyone has flashlights or headlamps. You will be amazed at the transformation of the sounds and smells; textures also change—such as the tree bark so hot in the afternoon now feels cool and moist; and, of course, the visuals completely change.

On a naturalist-led night hike at an eco-lodge in Costa Rica, one friend learned a "flashlight trick": Hold a flashlight parallel to your eyes, resting on your ear, and look around at the trees. What you will see is lots of pinpoints of light staring back at you. These are the eyes of spiders! It's magical!

But you don't have to go to Costa Rica to enjoy the outside world 24/7. You can do the spider exercise in your own backyard. In fact, there are many adventures close to your own porch that you may not have thought of until hiking made you more connected to the outside world. Here are my favorites to share with family, friends, and neighbors:

• Turn off your outside lights, stretch out on the ground, and watch the stars. If you know the constellations, point them out. Or be silly and make up constellations out of your own interpretations of the starry swaths above you. Give a name to your constellation and imagine a funny legend to go along with it.

• Tell campfire stories, myths, and legends—without the campfire.

• Come up with rhymes and poems inspired by the heavenly dome of night.

• Name as many songs as you can that have the words sunset, stars, or moon in them, and sing them if you can remember the tune and the lyrics.

• Pick a special star and keep it for your very own. Make a wish.

Wild Times

SPOTTING WILDLIFE IS ONE OF THE GREAT JOYS of hiking. You are in their territory now, and getting to know these creatures outside of books and zoos is always a thrill. Of course, this thrill-seeking must be conducted at all times at a good distance. Not only does this keep you safe, it protects the animals as well.

It's worth your time to gather as much information about area creatures and plant life as you can before your feet hit the trail. The more you know about the natural habitats of your destination, the more you will appreciate the reality show that surrounds you. The Internet makes it easy to quickly scan what is going on, animal- and plantwise, in your hiking region. Just 30 minutes or so at your computer can yield a wealth of basic facts that may surprise you. Such surfing can also can help you decide a focus, in case you want to spend money on a nature book that's of greatest interest to you. For example, you may learn that the area is teeming with migrating birds this time of year, and that is what really fires you up. So you would seek out a good guide on our feathered friends flocking to that area.

Then at state and national parks, most visitor centers have brochures and checklists of wildlife that you may see in the area. And it is almost always worthwhile to sign up for an excursion with rangers or naturalists before you set out on your own. They can give you more of the "inside scoop" about the park inhabitants (and about some of the local humans as well, perhaps).

I cannot stress enough how much difference it makes to have some real understanding of what you are looking at on your trails. For example, hiking in the Sonoran Desert, at Arizona's Saguaro National Park, is exciting in itself. And you would likely stop and admire the candelabra-shaped, namesake cactus. But to know that the saguaro (pronounced "sah-WAH-roh") matures at about age 125, typically lives to about age 200, and that in droughts its flesh feeds many different mammals, from jackrabbits to bighorn sheep, gives you a whole new appreciation for this icon of the Southwest. (And you will marvel at the estimation that only one in every 275,000 saguaro seeds will grow into a mature cactus.)

The WIDE, Wide, WIDE, Wide ECOLOGICAL World

Depending on where you decide to hike, you will likely encounter several ecologies and microclimates all in that one region. Here is a cursory look at what to expect in different areas:

IN THE FORESTS: I spend most of my hiking fun time in the woods. I read that a satellite view of the United States shows that 40 percent of the country is covered with these vast swaths of greenery. Trees are, of course, the building blocks of these forests: they add moisture to the air, provide shade on a warm day, and help remove pollution. Plus, they're nice to look at, they absorb noise, they cut down on wind, and they hold soil in place.

As you hike, you'll have many opportunities to study leaves and their various shapes, sizes, colors, and changes with the seasons. That's all part of the rewarding pursuit of learning to identify trees. I find their structures to be unending sources of intrigue. The trunk holds the life-support system, a foundation for the branches and the leaves. It is the tree's highway, allowing water and minerals to travel upward from the roots to the leaves, and food to travel downward for storage. These are the kinds of thoughts that hiking inspires in me, and I am sure it will in you as well.

The edges of forest are truly fascinating because of their crucial importance to wildlife. These borders between the forest and the meadow or waterway provide homes for many kinds of critters that can take advantage of the foods available in each. As you hike, keep your eyes peeled along the forest's edge for animal tracks, droppings, and nests. These indicate which animals have found shelter there.

Extinct vs. Endangered vs. Threatened

Some animals are doing better than we think, while others are quietly slipping close to extinction. As a hiker who loves the wilderness, you will want to keep up with this dynamic situation.

• *Extinct* speaks for itself: the species has gone the way of the, well, you know . . . the dinosaur.

• *Endangered* is very serious business. This means that the species is approaching extinction, and human ingenuity and protection is its only hope.

• *Threatened* denotes that we still have time to save the species—but not a lot of time.

Within the forest, look for as many shapes and types of leaves as you can. Leaves can be scalelike, needlelike, broad, or flat. They may be simple or compound; they may grow by themselves on a branch or a twig; or they may be made up of many leaflets. Find twigs that feel smooth, fuzzy, and thorny; twigs that are brown, green, black, red, or yellow. Get on the ground. Lie on your back under a tree. Look up and see what shapes the patterns of branches form. Look at the sky from here.

ALONG THE WATERWAYS: Water moves around the planet like a huge circulatory system, and wherever you hike you can see the cycle in action: clouds, rain, sleet, snow, oceans, rivers, ponds, even the lowly puddle. All of that water comes from somewhere, and it is going somewhere—either flowing or evaporating. It is the critical substance for all of life, and a natural force that you can observe during months, seasons, and years of hiking. Drop a stick or a leaf into a stream and follow it downstream: Where does it speed up, slow down, get caught? What other things float on the water? What happens to them? Look in pools along the edge. How do the creatures in a stream live here? Most have adapted to stay out of the areas of greatest current, have kept from being washed away. When you take time to stop and observe water, the questions can't help but flow into your mind.

BY THE POND: Watery environments such as ponds and lakes look tranquil, but they actually teem with life. Cattails and trees grow along the edge, but a complex order of life lies just below the surface and nearby.

When your hike leads you to a pond, you should definitely stop to explore. That's something best done by just sitting quietly and watching. It's so busy! In the mud along the edge of the pond, you'll see the tracks of deer, raccoons, and muskrats. On, in, and flying over the water, you'll see the frogs, ducks, muskrat, beavers, ripples from fish below, water striders on the surface, swallows, and herons. If you have a chance, take a boat onto the water, or lie on a dock and look into the water with a pondscope. (The Internet is loaded with ways to make your own pondscope out of a tin can, some plastic, and a few other standard household items. The main thing you need is a pond!) With a pondscope, you can glimpse into the universe of algae and insects beneath the water without much disturbance and without the glare from the water's surface. Kids love to do this—and they are great at making pondscopes!

BY THE SEA: Many find the seashore a great place for hiking vacations. For me, it's hard to not associate beach areas with sunbathing and a good book. But many parks and trails lead you to or along our oceans. Northern California's Point Reyes National Seashore and Maine's Acadia National Park are just two examples of spectacular oceanside settings riddled with trails. Among the Great Lakes, Wisconsin's Apostle Islands National Lakeshore, on Lake Superior, has trails that encompass lighthouses, beaches, and unforgettable overlooks. And we think of Caribbean islands for sailing, snorkeling, diving, and beaching, but there is some fantastic hiking to do there, island after island.

The seaside is a perfect place to tune in to natural happenings. Seaside plants and animals must adjust to constant changes if they are to survive. The shifting sands, winds, temperatures, and rainfall cause changes in living conditions on the seashore along with the constant fluctuations in tides and waves. Sandy beaches, sand dunes, estuaries, salt marshes, and rocky shorelines all offer ways to look at seashore life when your hiking leads you there. Just a few things, among many, to ponder:

- Note how wind and salt have affected trees and shrubs.
- Look for seabird tracks in the sand.
- Can you tell that waves are shaping the beach?
- Watch a tidepool.
- Turn over wet seaweed to see what's underneath (but disturb nothing!).
- Compare the colors of beach creatures, such as hermit crabs, with the surroundings.
- Collect sea glass.

IN THE DESERT: You may not always think "desert" when you take up hiking, but there is a lot to explore here—and some great trails. As hikers, we can visit four major deserts in the

Never, Never, Ever . . .

. . . feed wildlife. No matter how cute or how hungry the creature may look. The National Park Service is always broadcasting this warning in their literature. The folks at Hawai`i Volcanoes National Park really slammed it home, however, with their signage: A FED NENE IS A DEAD NENE. This is in reference to the state bird (pronounced "nay-nay"), a goose that is endemic to the islands. It was once near extinction, and it remains endangered. Tourists love to feed the nene, thus attracting the geese to the main roadways for more food, where they are then run over by tourists' cars. The park closes some roadways to protect the nene during nesting times, but hikers who register can still access the trails, so it's up to us to not ever feed these living treasures.

United States: the Mojave, Great Basin, Sonora, and Chihuahua. All are located in the western part of the country.

Hiking through a desert in the daytime may give you the impression that no animals are present. Since water is the primary requirement for life, each plant and animal has found efficient ways to capture and retain water. About 70 percent of desert animals spend the daylight hours underground to avoid heat, dryness, and predators. Therefore, most wildlife activity in the desert goes on between dusk and dawn. Take this as your cue and adjust your hiking schedule to be safe in this harsh, daylight environment. Bring plenty of water, more than you think you will need, when you set out on a desert trail. You'll also want astute clothing protection against temperature fluctuations (especially in high-desert country), sun exposure, and cactus spines.

ON THE PRAIRIE: As the early American settlers crossed the United States from the Atlantic to the Pacific coasts, the eastern tall-grass prairies gave way to shorter grasses in the more arid rain shadow of the Rocky Mountains. Today, the eastern tall-grass prairie lands have been plowed into the most productive agricultural belt on Earth; the western short-grass plains sustain ranching. So drastically has the landscape been changed that much of the native wildlife no longer exists.

In the middle of the United States, where less than 40 inches of rain falls each year, grasses that can survive drying winds and frequent droughts have become the dominant vegetation. That and plant-eating animals are what you will see when you hike in this part of the country. Among these herbivores are vast numbers of insects and rodents that are a basic link in the food chain. Be on the lookout, and listen out, for: prairie dog, cottontail rabbit, meadow vole, goldfinch, pocket gopher, grasshopper, harvest mouse, woodchuck, pronghorn antelope, jackrabbit, dickcissel songbirds, coyote, fox, red-tailed hawk, bull snake, meadowlark, garter snake, ground squirrel, cricket, burrowing owl, coyote, badger, praying mantis, ladybug, firefly, honeybee, monarch butterfly, and painted lady butterfly.

Family
Games

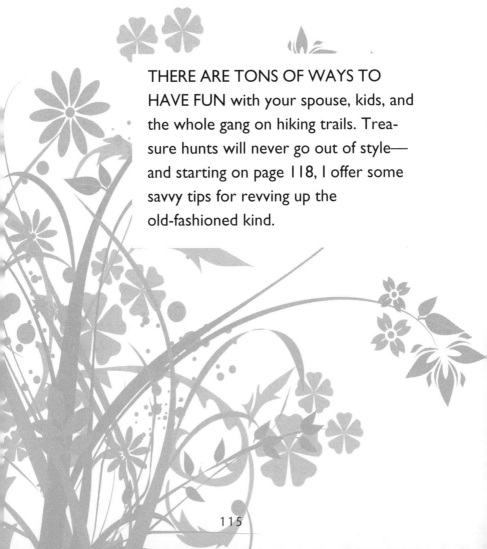

THERE ARE TONS OF WAYS TO
HAVE FUN with your spouse, kids, and
the whole gang on hiking trails. Treasure hunts will never go out of style—
and starting on page 118, I offer some
savvy tips for revving up the
old-fashioned kind.

But there's a whole new way to go on a treasure hunt these days, thanks to technology, and it's called geocaching. (It's kind of ironic that high-tech gear would get more of us into the ultimate low-tech place, the wilderness. Hmmm . . .) Anyway, whoever invented it understands that we never outgrow the thrill of playing hide-and-seek, or our fascination with the mystery and promise of treasure chests.

CATCH *on to* GEOCACHING

If you are new to this worldwide craze, you have a great hobby in store. You must have a GPS device to participate, but you can rent one at **www.lowergear.com** until you're sure you want it for keeps. And believe me, you will want your very own. Aside from fueling your newfound geocaching addiction, a GPS will greatly expand your hiking range and self-assurance on wilderness trails. But renting is a good way to learn how to use a GPS and figure out which bells and whistles you want—or don't want—on the one you buy. There is a huge price range, $100 to $1,000, so you don't want to pay for any features you can't imagine using.

Geocaching is a one-size-fits-all outdoor activity. Geocachers use GPS technology to locate close to 500,000 caches, or treasure boxes, hidden in nearly every country of the world. Their locations vary from busy downtown areas to remote caves. The "treasure" is usually a trinket or toy. You take something from the cache, leave something for the cache, and then add your name(s) to the cache's logbook.

Geocache tokens are limited only by size and your imagination, but you should never leave food or candy. Many people leave a geocoin—a metal coin minted and trackable on the Internet using a serial number and Web site engraved on the coin. A less expensive alternative is a geotoken. I like to gather a collection of personal tokens that I can

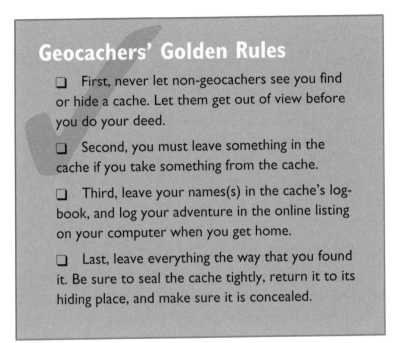

Geocachers' Golden Rules

❑ First, never let non-geocachers see you find or hide a cache. Let them get out of view before you do your deed.

❑ Second, you must leave something in the cache if you take something from the cache.

❑ Third, leave your names(s) in the cache's logbook, and log your adventure in the online listing on your computer when you get home.

❑ Last, leave everything the way that you found it. Be sure to seal the cache tightly, return it to its hiding place, and make sure it is concealed.

use at a moment's notice: polished rocks, charms, pencils, crystals, party favors, free ice cream coupons, and notes with inspirational messages.

GETTING STARTED: To find out if there are caches near you, log on to **www.geocaching.com** and enter your zip code. For the clues that can lead you to caches within a 10-mile radius, you will have to open an account, but you can open a basic one for free. With an account, you log in, then click onto a cache that sounds interesting, and the searchable database gives its *waypoints*. These are longitude and latitude coordinates that will look like this: N 47° 36.215 W 122° 19.767.

This information enables you to pinpoint the cache location in your GPS machine and translate that to the hike area and on to your prize. If you are familiar with the trails in your region, you may be able to tell approximately where the cache is hidden.

Each listing rates the cache's terrain and difficulty, which tells you how hard the area is to navigate, and how elusive the cache may be. Don't expect to see a spotlight and lighted arrow pointing you to the exact location, complete with a marching band! It's a little more complicated than that.

After you download the waypoints into your GPS, it routes you to the trail. Once you log the mileage and get within a radius of the waypoints, you may spend a while wandering around, looking in bushes and under rocks to find the actual cache. It is usually in a waterproof container, like an old ammo box, and should be easy to open.

LETTERBOXING

Letterboxing uses directions, clues, and riddles instead of the waypoints used in geocaching to locate treasures on a hike. At its simplest, a letterbox is a holder intended as a type of mailbox. At **www.letterboxing.org** you'll find instructions for making and hiding your own letterbox. Here you will also learn about assembling the rubber stamp, stamp pad, and other items you'll need for the game. The site also gives directions, clues, and riddles leading you to another person's hidden letterbox.

Once you find the hidden letterbox, you imprint yours or your family's stamp in the logbook inside the letterbox. Then you imprint your own logbook with the stamp stored inside the letterbox. It's an "I was here" sort of thing. This is an exciting process because the stamps you find can be quite creative, ranging from a simple return address to handmade works of art. Think of them as passports in the wilderness.

TREASURE HUNTS

These games have always been associated with children, but they work for engaging all ages on hikes. A treasure hunt does not require you to leave objects hidden in the wild, so it is in keeping with the Leave No Trace philosophy. (Many purists believe that geocaching and letterboxing do not adhere to Leave No Trace, as by their very nature, foreign objects are purposefully placed into the wild.)

A treasure hunt is traditionally conducted by handing out a list of items that might be seen on the hike—and ticking off each success. But another popular method is to make "treasure cards," with one item listed on each card. You can use them over and over, and make notes on the back when something unusual strikes you. A stack of index cards (green for nature?) is the perfect size, and they hold up. Instead of *writing* the object on the card, you or your kids can cut pertinent pictures from newspapers or magazines and paste them on. Some people even laminate their cards, punch a hole in the corner, and use a small carabiner to attach them to their packs. It's easy to add and subtract cards this way, and they are always handy for the next hike. You get the idea.

TREASURE-CARD CREATIVITY: Never hesitate to spice up this activity, especially if children are involved. The whole point is to encourage your group—young or old—to observe their surroundings. Activities that stimulate everyone's senses give fresh perspectives on any hiking trail. Here are some variations for treasure cards that my family likes:

• Adapt the game for your area. For example, include your state bird, or a sign showing a trail named after a local benefactor, or a path that leads to an abandoned water tower.

• Design your cards to require a response. For instance: Can you find an example of damage the last storm did in this forest? (See more examples in the boxes following.)

• Add sounds to the list—a train whistle in the distance, the high-pitched screech of a squirrel, the repertoire of a mockingbird. (See more examples in the boxes following.)

Kim's Treasure Trove

As you can see, I really enjoy the treasure-hunt game for group and family outings, and I want to share my tried-and-true lists with you.

What can you find that . . .

1. A bird would eat

2. Has a weird smell

3. Is the smallest thing you can see

4. Looks like an animal track

5. Chirps

6. Always changes

7. Erodes

8. Is an animal's home

9. Is shorter than everyone in the group

10. Is taller than everyone in the group

11. Has six legs

12. Likes sun

13. Sounds like a drum

14. Looks good enough to eat

• Play games like I Spy, and give points to the first person to see something on your treasure list or cards.

• Make number flash cards, and count really big rocks as you hike. (This works for little children.)

• Choose different themes for different seasons.

Tree treasure hunt . . .

1. Find a tree that has blossoms

2. Find a nest in a tree

3. Identify three things that trees need to grow

4. Take a photograph of a tree

5. Write a poem about a tree

6. Do a bark rubbing

7. Find the oldest tree

8. Find the youngest tree

9. Estimate the height of a tree

10. Find a tree that has changed something else

11. Identify different species of trees

12. Find a tree that smells like butterscotch

13. Find a dead tree

14. Identify a tree sound

15. Find a leaf that looks like a heart

• Keep a "trump card" tucked away for special sightings: bull snake, lost watch, or an abandoned sock. (If you find trash, be sure to pick it up and pack it out! That's another good reason to tuck a small garbage bag into your pack.)

Kim's Treasure Trove (continued)

Find . . .

1. A red car at the trailhead

2. A bird with blue markings

3. A hiker with a beard

4. A flying insect

5. A tree with pinecones

6. A waterfall

7. A mammal

8. A girl in a pink shirt

9. A green rock

10. A bird chirping

11. A squirrel

12. An abandoned cabin

13. An elk

14. A red-tailed hawk

15. A Colorado columbine wildflower

Touch something . . .

Rough

Smooth

Dull

Pointy

Soft

Hard

Bumpy

Squishy

Crumbly

Wet

Smell something . . .

Sweet

Sour

Flowery

Minty

Bad

Pinelike

Lemony

Fruity

Listen for . . .

Leaves rustling

Twigs snapping

Birds singing

Animals moving

Water running

Insects buzzing

Wind moving things

Picture-**Perfect**

AFTER YOU LOAD UP EVERYTHING for your outing, you may be reluctant to pack a valuable digital camera. So why not take a disposable digital camera or get a small, non-SLR (non–single lens reflex) for your "hiking camera." Or put the kids in charge of image collecting, if they are old enough. My kids love taking pictures outdoors, and I am always surprised at the variety I get back.

In practice, outdoor photography is a specialty all its own. Nature and wildlife photographers spend hours, days, weeks, walking through the backcountry, waiting and searching for the perfect shot. So don't be discouraged if your roll of photos or memory card is full of blurry close-ups of meadow wildflowers. Or the buffalo had turned his head before you clicked. Or the Douglas fir seems to be growing out of your husband's head.

Here are a few tips to ease whatever anxiety you have about taking snappy shots on the trail. Always keep in mind two things:

1. You cannot make a moose move into better lighting.

2. A photograph will never replace the memories of a sunrise on a particular trip, on a special day that you will always keep in your heart.

LIGHTING: Early morning and late afternoon are called the magic hours for good reason: the lighting is soft, and fewer shadows compete with your image. Absence of light and the dark of night also make for beautiful shots. A photograph of an elk prodding its young along a stream will have more appeal and a heavenly quality when a ray of sunshine kisses both of them. At noon, this same photography may be washed out with the light high and overhead.

THE RULE OF THIRDS: How do you capture an elusive rainbow or any landscape shot? Put it into perspective by placing an image in the foreground—perhaps a person or an interesting tree. Divide what you see in your frame into thirds and try to have an element of interest in each third. That way the picture is balanced and feels like the real vista. We rarely look at a land-scape and see only the lake. We also see what is on the lake, such as a boat, and what is around the lake, such as a mountain range or a deserted picnic table. Having a frame of reference always makes a photograph more interesting.

PEOPLE: You generally are not hiking alone, so take some shots of your companions during your journey. Don't get all strict and make them pose. Instead, watch their gestures and catch them in a moment. A photo of your friend looking at an interesting spider web is always better than a canned smile or snapshot of them standing in the middle of the trail.

A professional photographer I know of in Maine came up with a neat trick. He goes ahead and has people pose, and he clicks a couple of shots as expected. They hear the shutter release and think it's over. But when they relax from the pose, he clicks again, and that's when he gets the picture he wants. He also snaps their surprised faces when they realize he's still shooting. Fun!

KID CLICKS: I suggested you let your young family members take charge of the camera sometimes, and I want to bring that up again. They have such an interesting perspective. Sure, there will be plenty of pictures of backsides, but you also will have a treasure trove of new ways to see the trail. They usually take pictures from a different physical level and will always focus on things that are more organic and more candid.

CLOSE-UPS: As for the elusive wildflowers, a great rule of thumb is to get on their level. (Ditto for taking pictures of children.) Don't stand over a flower and snap away. Get on your knees, lie on your belly, and really get a shot. Macro and micro lenses are essential for close-ups of flowers and fauna. Many digital cameras have this capability without making a serious upgrade, so check on your camera's range.

Photographers call another wildflower trick "filling the frame." This means focusing so the wildflower or the flower and its immediate habitat occupy the entire picture.

Perspective is also important with close-up photography, so keep in mind that staging is okay. (You know, in the magazine world, stylists make things look, well, picture-perfect. And some nature photographers mist flowers with water to create dewdrop effects in their pictures.) So transfer a ladybug from one place to another if you would like to add character to a wildflower. (Then I suggest moving her back to her original location, just to be sure you haven't totally disrupted her life!)

What you do with all of your photographs is the rest of the story. Digital cameras offer instant gratification, but a system for keeping your hiking images organized is just as important as capturing the scene. Otherwise you'll never get around to enjoying them. Photo applications on personal computers make it relatively easy, as with Apple's iPhoto; if you own a Mac of fairly recent vintage, it's easy to create albums that, in themselves, give you efficient organization. You can print out the album; if you have Internet access, click on an iPhoto button to send the album electronically to Apple, where it will be made into a hardbound book; or simply let it sit in your "source list," perfectly organized. Sure beats hundreds of prints lying in a drawer somewhere!

To share your hiking experiences, turn your photos into a slide show (again, easily accomplished with personal-computer programs). Then show it to friends at a dinner party, or give a little nature talk at your son or daughter's school, or use it to convince women in your book club to join your hiking program!

CAMERA READINESS: If you are planning to shoot pictures while hiking, here are some reminders for take-alongs:
- Spare batteries and memory card(s)
- Instruction manual (if the camera is new to you)
- Lens cloth. This is really necessary if your camera is exposed to the outdoors a lot.

• Travel-sized tripod. Check out the spiffy Gorillapod (**www.joby.com/products/gorillapod**). It's available in three sizes, including a very small one. You can twist its three legs every which way, even wrap it around a tree limb or fence.

We ♥ Mother Earth

I'VE ALWAYS ADMIRED how the Girl Scout program teaches girls and teens to be sensitive to their surroundings. They commonly ask: How many people know the colors of the rainbow in order? What words would you use to describe a milkweed pod? When was the last time you saw a sunrise? Have you heard the call of an owl at dusk? Can you recognize your state's flower, bird, and tree in their natural settings?

Being a really good outdoor observer takes time to develop in us humans. Unlike animals that live wild in nature, we don't have to rely on our instincts every minute to get food and water, avoid predators, and survive. So our own sixth sense, or instinctive awareness, needs a little coaxing.

To me, it starts with respect for our land and water, and teaching others to do the same. Whether I am on a city, county, state, or national park trail, I try to remember that great care, as well as our tax dollars, have gone into creating these routes that allow us to get to know the outdoors. I try to be a good hiker citizen, and pass that on to my children by teaching them to

- Treat the trail, wildlife, and fellow hikers with respect
- Stay on existing trails—that is, don't make new trails of your own
- Observe trail and road closures
- Avoid trespassing on private land
- Obtain all permits and authorizations when required
- Pack out what you pack in, since Mother Nature has no trash-removal service
- Leave only footprints (Leave No Trace is an official program; see **www.lnt.org**)

According to the Wilderness Act of 1964, wilderness areas are "where earth and its community of life remain untrammeled, where man himself is a visitor who does not remain." Some mark is left in the outdoors and wilderness every time we visit, but each of us can make sure the mark is a small one.

(And, just in case you forgot, the colors of the rainbow, in order, are red, orange, yellow, green, blue, and purple.)

SPECIAL SECTION
Journaling the
Journey

"I have a notebook with me all the time, and I begin scribbling a few words. When things are going well, the walk does not get anywhere; I finally just stop and write."
—Mary Oliver, poet

THERE'S NOTHING LIKE SITTING ON A BIG ROCK on a beautiful trail and just letting words flow, higgledy-piggledy, onto our private pages. Surrounded by nature, we are inspired to nurture our own best selves. Sometimes that is painful, sometimes it is full of joy. But for me, it is a lifesaver.

I have come to understand more about my life as I hike than in any other single time or place. I know that to be true because for years I have been capturing my thoughts in journals that I've carried with me over every kind of terrain. Those pages show me who I am: Sometimes I don't like what I read, years later. Sometimes I laugh. Sometimes I think, "oh, brother." But I am always glad those feelings got authenticated in some way, just by being there in ink or pencil or whatever I had in my pack that would make a mark. There are outdoor journals that are compact and water-resistant, perfect for hiking, but I prefer art-supply sketch books. I like this way of writing, on plain white unruled paper, on the trail, away from the computer. I am less inclined to retype my thoughts, or to edit myself.

So join me on this journey, with your thoughts and observations and scribbles and sketches. Let the words flow! Write your secrets, just as when you were a little girl with your first diary and its precious key. Such pure creative freedom feels like you are shaking out the sheets in your adult mind.

Here are some exercises that will help you get started.

WARM UP!

• What do you want more than anything in your life? Why do you want it (two reasons)?

• How will you do/get it? Break it into small steps. Think *microhiking goals*.

• Write down the names of at least two people who will help you.

• Pick a start date and write it down now.

- How are you going to stick with it?

- How will you evaluate your success or the experience?

TAKE INVENTORY

Visualize symbols that represent your skills and talents and personality, and sketch or write these images in your journal. Or think of a stamp you could use in your journal that would be very specific to you. If you were a forest animal, what would you be? If you were a tree or flower, which would you be? If you were a hiking trail, would you be steep and difficult or paved and smooth? Do you associate a star with your leadership qualities, or a rainbow with your prosperity? Do you like red, which makes you feel courageous, or yellow, which makes you feel happy? You get the idea.

MAKE A NATURE CALENDAR

In an old issue of *FamilyFun* magazine, I saw an idea for a different kind of journal-keeping. It is a perpetual nature calendar, for tracing outdoor experiences and becoming more aware of all that is going on in nature. The technique is to gather a stack of 365 index cards; write a day of the year on each; take turns noting any natural observations or activities—"Saw our first rattlesnake," "Found a peculiar mushroom," and so on. Store the cards in a box and add to them every year for a nature-inspired record that grows with your family. You can create a similar nature diary in your journal.

YOUR LIFE MAP

In your journal, create a map that navigates how you are go-ing to deal with one issue in your life, or how you are going to accomplish some task—maybe the one you wrote about in the first exercise. Use your favorite colors and symbols and think of trail markers you can write or sketch in to show your progress.

CHILDHOOD MEMORIES

Write your memories of being a little girl and playing outside. What did you do? Who did you play with? What games did you play? How did you feel when you had to come inside?

HOW DO YOU FEEL RIGHT NOW?

How has your feeling changed about being outside since you were a child?

Deep down, are you frightened of the natural outdoors? Or does it make you feel free? What's the best thing that could happen to you in the outdoors? Close your eyes and think about how you feel. Channel those feelings onto paper: scribbles, doodles, drawings, pictures, colors, or words. When you are finished, look over what you have done. Look at this page a few days from now and write about your reaction to it.

MAP YOUR LIFE

Imagine your typical week or day or month. Think about all of the activities and functions that you perform, the roles you play, responsibilities you have, the things you like to do. Draw a large shape on the page and divide it into sections that represent each aspect of your life. Let each section reflect its importance through color, shape, size. What does it show that you would like to change? Make a new map of your life the way you want it to be.

NURTURE YOURSELF

Close your eyes and ask: How do I take care of myself?
Divide a page into three columns: Nurturing Places and
Things, Nurturing People, and Nurturing Activities. In each
column, list the items in your life that fit the category. Review
what you write from time to time to see if you are getting
out of balance with your priorities.

REFLECT ON YOUR BODY

Picture your body and take an inventory of your physical
sensations and feelings. Draw your body or write about your
body in an image of health and wellness just as you picture it
in your imagination.

PRIORITIES

Write a list of all the things you feel you *must* do (like schedule a business lunch). Next to that, write a list of all the
things you *want* to do (like see the new Brad Pitt movie).
Write about how your list makes you feel.

YOUR SUPPORT SYSTEM

Write the names of the people that you turn for understanding, encouragement, support, or assistance. Study this support system carefully. If you see a need to strengthen your
network by adding to it or enriching it, write down ways in
which you will go about doing this.

YOUR FAVORITE THINGS

Think about the things you *really* like. Not the things you
are *supposed* to like. Not the things people *think* you like.
But what do you *really* like? Think about the results. Are you

surprised? Write about why you think it appeals to you. How did it come into your life?

MY OWN SPACE

Picture the environment where you live, and draw a floor plan. Pretend you are a visitor there for the first time, and write down your impressions. Be honest. Do the same for your car or your office.

REVIEW YOUR JOURNEY

Take a look at the work that you've done through your hiking, journaling, and self-discovery. Has writing in your journal, in tandem with hiking, helped you

• Express candid feelings and thoughts?

• Find deeper meaning in your life?

• Enrich your relationship with yourself, others, and nature?

• Define and implement life changes?

• Make more conscious choices and decisions?

• Sort out challenges in your life?

Women have been trained to speak softly and carry a big lipstick. Those days are over.
—Bella Abzug

PART FIVE

FOR WOMEN ONLY

Bathroom
Breaks

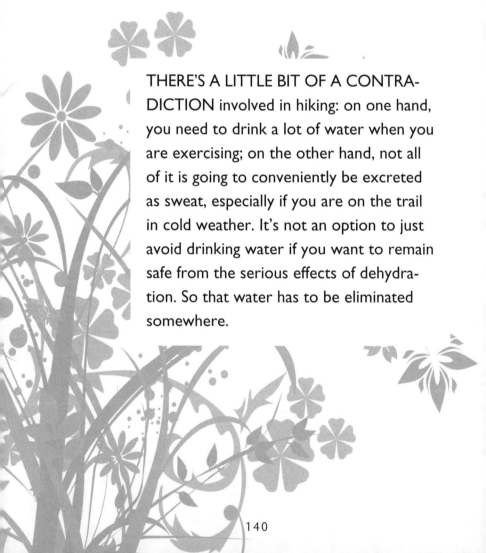

THERE'S A LITTLE BIT OF A CONTRA-
DICTION involved in hiking: on one hand,
you need to drink a lot of water when you
are exercising; on the other hand, not all
of it is going to conveniently be excreted
as sweat, especially if you are on the trail
in cold weather. It's not an option to just
avoid drinking water if you want to remain
safe from the serious effects of dehydration. So that water has to be eliminated
somewhere.

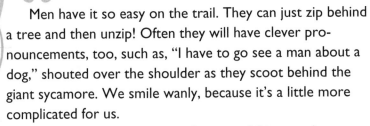

Men have it so easy on the trail. They can just zip behind a tree and then unzip! Often they will have clever pronouncements, too, such as, "I have to go see a man about a dog," shouted over the shoulder as they scoot behind the giant sycamore. We smile wanly, because it's a little more complicated for us.

In fact, I know of women who resist hiking much more than an hour's walk in the park due to the toilet topic. If anyone feels that way who is reading this book, I hope I can get you reconsider, put this into perspective, and get out on longer treks.

Aside from the more developed hiking trails, you'll find no bathrooms on your hike. Trailheads sometimes have a pit toilet, but don't count on it. Whether you find yourself traveling with your monthly period, have a bladder-control concern, or just have to pee, you of course want to be prepared. And it's not that hard to do.

Bring along with you a few sheets of toilet paper—or one of those convenient travel packs—and a small, plastic, sealable-top bag for carrying out the soiled tissue. If you do get into a situation of having to wipe with a nearby leaf, you won't ever want to do that again. (Yes, there have been cases of people unwittingly using poison oak leaves for toilet tissue, and it's not a pretty story.)

As with tissue, the same goes for tampons or pads. Bring them with you, and never leave them behind—not even under the bushes or leaves where you think it won't matter. It does. Many women rely on panty liners to catch accidents. You never know when you are going to cough, sneeze, or get the giggles—all motions that can release a little leak. (Those of us who have gone through childbirth a time or two know all about that.) I'd rather be safe than sorry, so feminine necessities are a staple in my hiking pack.

Back to the fact that we can't just run behind the tree and relieve ourselves standing up, like that other gender. (Well, there are products designed to help us remain vertical and pee, but it takes a while to get the hang of using them without creating a big mess. Some women swear they can use their fingers on their genitalia to direct the flow, man-style, but that's kind of tricky.)

Generally, we have to squat for everything toilet-related in the wilderness. This is another good reason for getting into good hiking shape, so those thigh muscles give you pain-free support as you suspend your body in a zigzag fashion for prolonged seconds or even minutes. Regarding this time-honored position, here are some words of caution, gained from my own experience and that of my female hiking buddies:

• Look for spots well off the trail, but still within easy shouting distance of your companion(s). A large bush, forested enclosure, group of boulders, or a cluster of tall cacti will spare your companions and other trail traffic a glimpse of the "moon."

• Look for a shrub branch, tree limb, or nearby rock that you could use if you need to steady yourself as you squat and then rise. It is crucial, however, that you don't pick just any plant-kingdom species for this helping hand. Be sure the bush or limb has no thorns, as they may be hard to see, and sometimes the leaves will have subtle spikes. One friend tells of her first Alaskan hiking adventure, when she unwittingly grabbed onto what appeared to be a handy branch, concealed by large leaves. The pain was instantaneous, because she'd connected to *Oplopanax horridus,* the plant Alaskans love to hate so much that they call it "devil's club." So assess the entire bush before you reach.

Avoiding Diarrhea

If you have a touch of diarrhea or stomach flu, you should probably stay home, close to your own facilities. But one way to avoid intestinal upsets on the trail is to always drink your own safe, carried water. Just as you don't want your canine hiking companion to lap water from springs and puddles because of the risk of giardiasis (see "Woman's Best Friend," on page 89), you shouldn't drink it, either. Though the damage from giardiasis may not strike until one to four weeks after ingestion, when it comes on it will have you shivering with chills and living in the bathroom with diarrhea and vomiting. Not only that, but it takes months to get your system back to normal. Trust me—I've had it, and it's horrible. Other waterborne parasites to worry about include E. coli and cryptosporidium, both of which are harder to kill than giardia.

• Scan your selected area for wild creatures and errant twines of poisonous plants. To alert animals, shuffle your feet and hum a little tune. In snake country, cast an eagle eye across your entire "bathroom," and keep humming!

• Use your boot to dig an indentation, or "cat hole," for pooping, and cover up the bounty when you finish.

• You probably wouldn't do this, but I'll say it anyway, especially because you may have to teach it to your daughter or other little girl: never sit directly on the ground in the outdoors.

As a last resort, you can always use the method that my sister employs. She waits until she gets home—no matter what. Her otherwise blue eyes could be green with the need to go, and she will wait.

QUICK-CHANGE ARTISTRY: Being grungy is not a trail requirement. You don't have to give up on personal hygiene just because there is no running water. Baby wipes and hand sanitizer in a small container are great for cleanup as well as germ control. If I am going to run an errand after I've been on the trail, I take a mini–sponge bath with such products. For a more complete makeover, you don't have to carry more "stuff" with you on the trail. Just have deodorant, lip gloss, mascara, a fresh top, maybe a skirt, and street shoes back in the car, and transform yourself at the park-entrance restroom, if there is one. If not, you can do it surreptitiously in your car. You'll head off for your burger feeling fresh as a daisy. Well, mostly.

Pregnancy **and** *Hiking*

PREGNANT WOMEN CAN HIKE into their third trimester if they are healthy, were in shape before they became pregnant, and were hiking before pregnancy. Each mother-to-be's doctor or midwife must give the go-ahead and, as always, let common sense be your guide.

After three children, I have some pretty firm beliefs about pregnancy. One is to exercise, move, walk, and hike. Of course, you'll need to maintain other healthful practices to *feel* like exercising. I always aimed for really good naps and overnight sleep to stay rested. I ate several small meals during the day and satisfied every craving. To settle my stomach, I took Tums, ate bananas, and wore Sea-Bands for morning sickness. ("Morning sickness," by the way, is a ridiculous term since the urpy feeling is usually 24/7.)

Along with hiking and a lot of snowshoeing, I used yoga and creative visualization. I felt like a goddess. After all, I was growing a human being, for goodness' sake! But don't let anyone—doctor, friend, relative—push you into something that you are not comfortable with. One pregnant friend felt pressured into a strenuous hike. She blamed the hike and her friend on a miscarriage a few weeks later. They were not connected, but the mental damage was done.

Make sure you have a plan for three months and more after the baby is born. In reality, pregnancy lasts more than nine months, because your body continues to go nuts for a while. Not only are you caring for your newborn, but you are also caring for your postpartum body and mind. Get someone to watch the baby for a few hours and go on a hike.

It is not advisable to take newborns out in the wild, but short walks in a stroller or a baby carrier are wonderful sensory experiences for the child and bonding opportunities for you both. As a new mother, I liked to hold my infant and walk around our yard and point out leaves, trees, flowers, and birds. These little walks initiated my child's perception of the outside world, and it was a calming experience for both of us. As the weeks and months flew by, I would take my children out in a stroller or baby carrier for more sensory and bonding opportunities.

So unless medical conditions require strict bed rest or severely limited physical activity, pregnancy or having a newborn baby shouldn't prevent you from getting outdoors. You will soon resent the whole situation if you feel cooped up. It may take a little creativity to stick to a hiking schedule as a pregnant woman or new mom, but I am proof that it can be done. Having a child is one of the most amazing things you will ever do, and your happiness is the cornerstone of your baby's life.

On *the* Trail *with* Your Offspring

MY SON AND TWO DAUGHTERS started hiking in Colorado before they were born. We hit the trail at least once a week while each baby was safe and sound in my womb. After that, he or she was inside the baby carrier and then the mega-dual-wheeled jogging stroller. The kids soon found their footing and began to do easy local walks.

Short Striders

INFANT TO 2 YEARS OLD: You'll be carrying or strolling them. Baby backpacks, baby carriers, strollers, bike trailers, and similar inventions provide baby and parent with ample opportunity to head out for paved trails or well-maintained gravel paths. And all this mobile-baby gear makes it easy to stash essentials such as diapers and baby wipes.

2 TO 4 YEARS OLD: Up to 2 miles with frequent stops and breaks to examine things that absorb their interest.

5 TO 7 YEARS OLD: Around 3 to 4 miles over easy terrain. You'll want to give them a slightly wide berth for running from here to there to observe things.

8 TO 10 YEARS OLD: A full day, at a slow pace (which you'll have to moderate, as they will start off at a gallop!). You can likely cover 6 miles over variable terrain. Starting in this age group, you can consider assigning a hiking leader (or mountain leader as we call it) and have that child guide the hike. Have your child invite a friend to come on the adventure, and have him take turns with her as the leader. This helps your child see the world from another youngster's perspective.

PRETEENS AND TEENS: If they are energetic kids and in good health, they can keep up with most active adults for a good day's outing. They still need to build experience for a long haul over difficult terrain.

Note: *Set your entire group or family hiking goals based on the youngest child's ability, and make sure that no child ever walks or runs beyond the immediate sight and easy grasping distance of at least one adult.*

In time, hiking became a great way to introduce the kids to insects, leaves, pinecones, wind. It's low-cost entertainment for them, and perfect for those cash-strapped times we all have when we have little ones. Over the years, we've developed many types of observation activities that absorb all of us on our strolls through nature (see "Family Games," on page 115). And it's great exercise for the whole family, without having to pay sports-club fees or stick to gym or pool schedules. Those activities are important, too, but hiking can be more a freewheeling, we're-in-the-mood type of family outing. And vacations centered around hiking can be as much (or more) fun than playing on the beach. A friend's two pre-teen children anticipate the family's annual trip to the Smoky Mountains all year long. They discuss the various trails, argue over which one to do first next year, and ask when they'll be old enough to tackle the long way up Mount LeConte.

Whether you're heading out on an off-the-cuff getaway or a family vacation, you can't overlook planning when hiking with children, early on, to teach them the routine. Where to hike, what to bring, safety factors, and how to keep the hike fun all go into making this kind of family time succeed.

Regarding pacing, don't think that a 5-year-old is ready to hike to the top of the glacier. Don't be disappointed if that same 5-year-old will go hiking only if she can wear her high-heeled glitter shoes. One acquaintance's 9-year-old daughter still insists on completing her hiking ensemble with pink sparkly boat shoes from the Gap. At this age, she and her mom negotiate which walks call for boat shoes (not many) and which call for athletic shoes or hiking boots (most of them). At least she *wants* to hike. We adapt to such challenges, and the kids learn to adapt to nature.

The guidelines in "Short Striders," on page 148, reflect my own experience and that of my friends for distances you can reasonably expect little legs to walk.

PACKING FOR THE KIDS: For starters, make a big deal about buying a small backpack for them to carry their own stuff. Spend time with them looking at different packs and trying them on for size. Engage in conversation about what they'll need and want in their packs. This gives the kids ownership of the process and parents don't end up schlepping everything for the entire family.

As for items in the packs, when hiking day arrives, that part is much like packing for the parents. Assuming the kids are with one or both parents, they won't have to carry everything that is *highly recommended* in the Hiker's Dozen, the hiking essentials listed on page 56. But their packs will be similar. Mom or Dad can certainly plan to carry knives and matches, and the kids won't have to. Also, the parent(s) will need to make sure that the younger children are adequately sprayed and layered up with insect repellent and sunblock.

DRESSING UP AND DOWN: Be sure everyone is dressed for the weather. You know the rule: layers! I joked about sparkle shoes before, and this is OK for a short little stroll if it makes your child happy. But for a real walk, all children need to proper socks and shoes. For the socks, as mentioned for your grown-up versions, avoid cotton, which does not wick

Top-5 Checklist for Little Backpacks

- ❑ Water
- ❑ Whistle
- ❑ Food
- ❑ Extra clothing for layering up and down (jacket, sweater, or rain protection; hat)
- ❑ Small flashlight

ADD-ONS FOR OLDER KIDS

- ❑ Map*
- ❑ Compass
- ❑ Sun protection (parents carry for younger kids)
- ❑ Insect repellent (ditto)
- ❑ First-aid kit
- ❑ Activity items such as treasure-hunt cards, magnifying glass, camera

Involve the family in making a special kid-friendly map, which doubles as a creative way to teach directions. Draw icons for waterfalls, trails, trees, rest areas, and such. Draw the route and have the child mark interesting way points during the hike.

moisture and can facilitate blisters. Instead, buy child-sized wool socks and nylon liners. Sturdy athletic shoes, with good arch supports, are fine, and child-sized hiking boots are even better.

SAFETY: There are several non-negotiable rules when hiking with kids, and the first one is that children must always stay within sight of an adult. (An acquaintance's preteen son died in the Smoky Mountains when he ran ahead of the family and fell down a ravine.) Here are the rules I give my kids or any other youngsters in my care on a hike:

• Always stay within eyesight of an adult.

• Never run ahead on the trail.

• Never hike off the trail. (Not only can kids get lost or injured, they also can cause damage to the trail.)

• Never go near steep cliffs or other drop-off areas.

• Stay back from rivers and other water sources.

• Climb on accessible rocks only with permission. (My answer is usually "NO!")

• Stay where you are, in one spot, if you think you are lost. Many children relate to hugging a tree, and you can teach them to do this if they get lost. Instruct them to find a tree on the trail, hold on, and blow their whistle. Three whistle blows is the standard distress signal and indicates: I am lost, or I need help.

I don't mean to scare you with tales of the trapped hiker who had to cut off his arm (page 81) or trail fatalities due to murder (page 171) or falling trees (page 163), but these are the realities of outdoor adventure. In two of these cases, a companion hiker may have made a difference; in the case of the child, if he had just stayed with his parents . . . But as you know, the statistics for driving a car or crossing the street can be equally harrowing.

ETIQUETTE: I also teach my children trail etiquette, and that if they treat the outdoors kindly, the outdoors will repay the favor:

• Leave no trace.

• Pick up after others who leave litter, if you can.

• The uphill hiker has the right of way.

• Don't pick or pull any growing thing.

• "Leaves of three, let them be." (This little ditty refers to poison oak, poison ivy, and poison sumac. The oak and ivy have three leaves originating from the same point on the stem, but sumac may have more.)

At the end of the day (literally), consider heading home a little early if the hike is going well. Better to end on a positive note than to face sore feet, a lot of whining, and that familiar refrain, "Are we home yet?"

Aging and Hiking

AS MY GRANDFATHER AGED, he spent time in the outdoors and adjusted his routine to adapt to his changing body. Since he lived right outside of Rocky Mountain National Park, he walked every day through the pine trees and past the elk that bedded down by his house. When he used a cane, he still got around outside. When he was in a wheelchair, my aunt would take him into the national park and help him along the trails that accommodated wheelchairs. He was an inspiration to me.

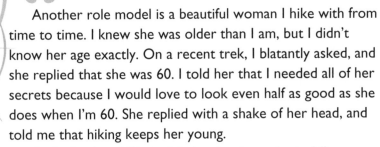

Another role model is a beautiful woman I hike with from time to time. I knew she was older than I am, but I didn't know her age exactly. On a recent trek, I blatantly asked, and she replied that she was 60. I told her that I needed all of her secrets because I would love to look even half as good as she does when I'm 60. She replied with a shake of her head, and told me that hiking keeps her young.

And why does hiking minimize the signs of aging? I'm not just talking about superficial looks. I'm thinking more of the real indicators of living with vitality into our later years. Well, the answer is that hiking, like any exercise, stimulates our circulation (aiding blood pressure), strengthens our heart muscle (reducing the risk of heart attack), increases our flexibility, and boosts our lung power. It helps us to not descend into the infamous "spread" of weight gain. And it reduces stress, which keeps our minds receptive to new things. All of that adds up to a glow that a table full of cosmetics just can't beat.

That's enough proof and incentive for me. I plan to be on the trail long past 60!

> Nature has no mercy at all. Nature says, "I'm going to snow. If you have on a bikini and no snowshoes, that's touching. I am going to snow anyway.

—Maya Angelou

PART SIX

MAMA
SAID
THERE'D
BE DAYS
LIKE THIS!

Wicked **Weather** and *Natural* **Hazards**

I CANNOT STRESS ENOUGH the effect weather has on your hiking trips. Be prepared for anything: sun, snow, lightning, hail, flash floods, and more. Start by knowing the weather forecast and the road conditions. That will help you pack smart. It can be a lovely day where you live but, especially in mountain regions, a trailhead may be inaccessible due to an approaching blizzard. Or a steep trail will be slippery if it is muddy or icy from recent storms or snow. If your hiking region is prone to natural disasters, that's another factor to weigh when you're thinking "wilderness."

It's a good idea to know the climate overview for brackets of time (say, for the summer) and the average temperature highs and lows in your hiking area. This data is readily available on the Internet and through local authorities; guidebooks can give you a weather overview, but you need to get current info.

Weather-watching in areas where you hike can be fun, almost like a game—though a very serious one. What does the barometric pressure have to do with your hike today? What is the significance of different wind speeds? What do cloud formations and changes in sky color tell you?

Following is a roundup of Mother Nature's furies that can affect your hiking plans. The impact can range from a minor inconvenience to a life-threatening emergency.

LIGHTNING: Violent storms are common in June, July, and August, and lightning usually strikes the tallest object in the area. At the first sign of a storm with lightning, find shelter. Nearby buildings or automobiles are safe places to seek refuge during the storm. Stay away from tall, solitary objects such as trees and electrical poles. Avoid barren hilltops and exposed areas. Get away from water. Avoid touching anything made of metal, such as a wire fence, and crouch low to the ground in exposed areas if no shelter is available.

Get an early start on all hikes that go above the tree line. Try to reach high-altitude summits by 1 p.m. and do a 180 when the weather turns bad. If you're caught in a lightning storm above tree line, stay off ridgetops. Spread out if you are in a group—but remain within sight of each other. Squat or sit with your feet together (on a foam pad if you are camping and have one in your sleeping gear). If someone is struck, be prepared to use CPR to help restore their breathing and heartbeat.

TORNADOES: Immediately seek shelter. If you are in an open field, lie down in the nearest ditch. A tornado is very dangerous because of its powerful and destructive force. A telltale funnel cloud, thick storm clouds, strong winds, lightning, hail, or dark skies all may signal an impending tornado. If a tornado warning is issued for the area you will hike, use common sense and stay away.

If you need protection from a tornado, safe places are storm shelters, basements, caves, tunnels, and reinforced buildings with hallways. But you are hiking, and these alternatives may be far away. So move away from the angle of the tornado's path, lie flat anywhere you can (such as a ravine, culvert, or ditch), and protect your head. Don't take shelter in a tent or your car, as these structures will probably be knocked around in a tornado, and are potentially very dangerous.

WINTER STORMS: These weather patterns include blizzards, heavy snowstorms, and ice storms. When you are hiking during the winter months, or shoulder seasons, be sure to have plenty of supplies and clothing layers. If you are caught unexpectedly in a winter storm, seek shelter and conserve body heat. Huddle with your buddy, and seek help together. Know the prevention techniques and first aid for hypothermia and frostbite (see "First Aid," page 173).

SWIFT WATER: Mountain streams can be dangerous during high snow runoff in May and June. Even a narrow stream may be deep and fast, as well as cold. Remain back from the banks of streams and rivers, especially if you cannot see the bottom. Provide extra-cautious supervision for children, as they tend to be attracted to water. Rocks at streamside and in the stream are often slippery, and water beneath them may be deep, so avoid stepping on them. Powerful currents can pull you under water and pin you below the surface.

Be careful when crossing streams, especially during a storm or a heavy runoff. Whether you are fording the stream or crossing on a log, make every step count. If you have any doubt about maintaining your balance on a foot log, go ahead and ford the stream instead. When fording a stream, use a trekking pole or stout stick for balance and *face upstream* as you cross. If a stream seems too deep to ford, turn back. Whatever is on the other side is not worth risking your life.

FLOODS: Watch for them after heavy rains, prolonged rains, or the occasional dam rupture. The National Weather Service provides flood alerts and warnings. If you are hiking and hear a warning, immediately evacuate the area. If that is not possible, climb to higher ground and wait for rescue personnel. Be prepared for this emergency if you are hiking in an area with a history or potential of flooding. Make sure, of course, to pack extra food, water, warm waterproof clothing, a flashlight, and a cell phone.

By definition, flash floods can occur unexpectedly at any time, and they are extremely dangerous because of deadly swift currents. Normally areas prone to flash flooding have signs warning of the danger, so always locate and plan your *upward* escape route before heading onto the trail. If a flash flood occurs, immediately run uphill to higher ground! Don't try to go back down the trail: *You will never be able to outrun a flash flood.*

HURRICANES: If there is a hurricane warning in the area you will be hiking, stay away from beaches and other locations that may be swept by storm waves. Watch for high water, as streams and rivers will commonly flood after heavy, hurricane-powered rains. Try to get indoors if you are caught in the elements, or at the very least, seek shelter in nature. When you think the worst has passed, be aware that winds from the other direction of the storm's eye could pick up. After the storm, do not hike in disaster areas, and watch for hazards such as dangling wires, undermined roads, flooded low spots, or fires.

AVALANCHES: When in snow-packed backcountry, avoid steep slopes and gullies where avalanches occur. Open slopes of 30 to 45 degrees can be loaded with dangerous masses of snow, easily triggered by the presence of one or more travelers. To learn current snow conditions, check with the weather service and, in parks, at the visitor centers.

EARTHQUAKES: If you are faced with an earthquake, remember that the biggest danger from this natural disaster is falling debris. If you are hiking near a known fault line and you've unmistakenly been in an earthquake, the best action is to keep calm. Undeveloped or treeless areas are beacons for earthquake safety, so you can be relieved that you were not in a city high-rise area.

WILDFIRES: If you are caught in a forest fire during a hike, you must get out as quickly as possible. If you haven't been alerted to a forest fire in the news, your nose will spot it for you: where there is smoke, there is fire. Head away from the smoke and avoid compromised areas, even after a fire has been contained. If you think you may have started a fire by accident, try to extinguish it by any means possible. When it looks as if you need assistance, report the fire to the nearest authorities as soon as possible.

Wildfires are becoming much more common because of drier soil, dry leaves and undergrowth, and less rainfall in some regions. The presence of warmer air produces more lightning that can touch off fires in delicate areas. It is important to know the conditions of the area you will be hiking in.

Has there been a drought? Are the temperatures higher than normal? Is it windy? All of these factors can lead to or help spread a wildfire.

If you indeed get caught within smell of, or—much worse—sight of, a wildfire, get to an area free from vegetation that has little to offer to fuel the fire: any body of water (lake, stream, pond); a road; rocky terrain. In any of these land refuges, move toward the middle. *Fires usually travel uphill, so try to get downhill and outrun the fire.*

DEAD OR DAMAGED TREES: Standing dead trees and storm-damaged living trees pose a real hazard to hikers. It really hit close to home with me, because a falling tree killed a hiker on one of my favorite trails one week after I was there. We noted on my hike that the trees seemed to lean and creak and that many of them had died and seemed to be trying to fall. In the fatal case, the hiker was with a buddy when the tree fell and hit him in the head—killing him and injuring his buddy.

To exercise caution, observe the trees around you as you hike, and as you seek spots for rest. Ditto when you pick a patch to pitch your tent, if you are camping. Dead and damaged trees may have loose or broken limbs that could fall at any time. If you are hiking in an area prone to storms or where storms recently occurred, be sure to listen for other falling trees and avoid these trails when it is windy. Remember: *Look up!*

Pests **and** *Growling* **Beasts**

HIKING OPENS THE DOOR to the animal kingdom in its natural habitat. In most cases, that is part of the charm of the sport. But we all know that, to us humans, some fauna are troublesome, at best, and dangerous, at worst. This wildlife tour travels from the smallest to the largest creatures of concern:

HANTAVIRUS: Minuscule agents that live on rodents cause the Sin Nombre hantavirus, which you catch simply by breathing dust where the hosts have lived. Beware of old cabins, mine shafts, caves, and ruins that shelter rodents, and don't tread where you see mouse burrows and droppings. Hantavirus can be a very serious illness, leading to kidney damage or failure.

MOSQUITOES: Bites from this creature are itchy, unpleasant, annoying, and can lead to illness. While not common, West Nile virus is transmitted by infected mosquitoes and humans are susceptible to the disease. Culex mosquitoes, the primary variety that can transmit West Nile virus, thrive in urban rather than natural areas. They lay their eggs in stagnant water and can breed in any water that stands for longer than five days. Most people infected with West Nile virus have no symptoms of illness, but some may become ill, usually 3 to 15 days after being bitten.

In most areas, August and September are the high-risk periods for West Nile virus. At this time of year—and any-time you expect mosquitoes to be buzzing around—wear protective clothing such as long sleeves, long pants, and socks. A loose fit and light colors are most effective. Spray clothing with insect repellent. Carefully follow the instructions on the product and take extra care with children. (Also see "Go Shopping!" in Part Two of this book.)

By all means, if you are riddled with mosquito bites, take an antihistamine and use anti-itch cream often—especially if you are going to be outdoors for a couple of days. Mosquito bites can easily become infected and cause unwanted grief on the trail.

TICKS: These suckers often wait on brush and tall grass to hitch a ride on a warm-blooded passerby. They love dark, warm places—like your scalp. A favorite ploy is to drop from a tree and nest in your hair. I've had many in my scalp and when I ran my fingers along the spot—well, let's just say you can't mistake a blood-sucking tick. I even looked at my sister one time to see what she had in her eye and it was a tick embedded in her eyelash!

While ticks are most visible in my area of Colorado in early- and midsummer, you should be on the lookout for them throughout spring, summer, and fall. Among our local varieties, deer ticks and dog ticks can transmit diseases, but both need several hours of attachment before they can transmit any harbored diseases. *Note that deer ticks, the primary carrier of Lyme disease, are very small, sometimes the size of a poppy seed.*

You can use several strategies to reduce your chances of tick trouble. Some people wear light-colored clothing, so ticks can be spotted before they make it to the skin. Insect repellent containing DEET is an effective deterrent. Most importantly, though, be sure to check yourself at the end of the hike. Ticks may settle into shoes, socks, and hats, and may take several hours to latch on. And if it's prime tick season, you may want to perform a quick check every hour or so.

Ticks that haven't attached are easily removed, but not easily killed. If you pick off a tick in the woods, just toss it aside. If you find one on your body at home, dispatch it and then send it down the toilet. For ticks that are already embedded, removal with tweezers is best. You must however, make sure that you get the entire tick—head, legs, and all—out of your skin.

FIRE ANTS: Here is one more reason to hike in boots or, for short walks, sturdy outdoor shoes that provide foot coverage and protection. Especially in some coastal areas, it is so easy to unwittingly step into a fire-ant hill, and the outcome is not pleasant if you are wearing sandals—even today's sturdy, popular waterproof types. If you insist on this footwear, then by all means carry some topical Benadryl or other analgesic. (I say "topical," because the pill form can make you drowsy.)

SPIDERS: The most dangerous spider in the United States is the black widow. Black widows may also be red or brown, and its famous hourglass pattern on the abdomen may be pronounced or not. When bitten, you may see swelling or redness at the bite; or you may suffer painful and prolonged muscle cramps. In severe cases, hospital treatment is required. The brown recluse spider, also called the violin spider because of the distinctive mark on the back, is another species of concern. If you are bitten by a spider, stay calm, ice the spot as soon as possible to reduce pain, and get help.

SCORPIONS: Related to spiders, these arachnids sting with their tails. Scorpion venom attacks the nerves but is unlikely to kill a healthy adult. Take note, desert hikers: the most dangerous species is the bark scorpion, found only in Arizona and immediately across the border in California. Though some scorpions are as long as eight inches, bark scorpions are less than half that length. They are yellow to yellowish green and have long, narrow pincers.

CENTIPEDES: These arthropods live mostly under rocks and in downed wood. Some have a nasty sting. Harmless millipedes, sometimes confused with centipedes, have two pairs of legs growing from each body joint while the centipede has just one.

BEES: This common group of insects is relatively harmless to most people, but their stings can produce serious anaphylactic reactions in others. I am allergic to bees, and an injection of epinephrine is a lifesaver for me. An allergic reaction is unmistakable: within a few moments, you can become faint and unable to breathe. If you have this allergy, always carry an epinephrine injector (EpiPen), and be sure your hiking buddies know about your reactions to bee stings. Show them the injector and how to use it—it's a simple jab in the thigh.

SNAKES: Most snake encounters for hikers will be with garter snakes, water snakes, and bull snakes (while not venomous, they are rather large and scary-looking). The only venomous snake in my area is the rattlesnake, and sightings are common. A good rule of thumb is to give them a wide berth. If you are bitten by a rattlesnake, stay calm and get help immediately.

If you are terrified of snakes, keep in mind that places like Hawaii and Rocky Mountain National Park are supposedly snake-free. Rocky Mountain National Park is very proud to claim that there is only one reptile inside the park and it's the harmless garter snake. This is not to say that there are not venomous snakes in areas that border the park region. (And have the reptiles gotten word that the park is snake-free, so they won't slither over?)

BEARS: There are no definite rules about what to do if you meet a bear. In most cases, the bear will detect you first and run off. If you do spot a bear nearby, here are some suggestions from the National Park Service (NPS):

1. Stay calm.
2. Talk loudly, to alert the bear to your presence.
3. Back away while facing the bear.
4. Avoid eye contact.
5. Give the bear plenty of room to escape; bears will rarely attack unless they are threatened or annoyed.
6. Don't run or make sudden movements; running will provoke the bear, and you can't outrun a bear.

7. Do not attempt to climb trees to escape bears, especially black bears. The bear may pull you down by the foot!
8. Fight back if you are attacked. Bears have been driven away when people have fought back with rocks, sticks, binoculars, and even their bare hands.

MOUNTAIN LIONS: Lion attacks on people are rare, with fewer than 12 fatalities in 100 years. Based on observations by people who have come in contact with mountain lions, some patterns are beginning to emerge. Here are more suggestions from the NPS:

1. Stay calm.
2. Talk firmly to the lion. (I'm not sure I understand the NPS goal here, but I guess if you're saying "Bad lion, no soup for you today," then you're being firm without becoming a screaming maniac.)
3. Move slowly.
4. Back up or stop. Never run, because lions will chase and attack.
5. Make yourself look bigger: Raise your arms or, if you are wearing a sweater or coat, open it and hold it wide.
6. Pick up children to make them appear larger.
7. If the lion becomes aggressive, throw rocks and large objects at it. This is the time to convince the lion that you are not prey and that you are a danger to it. Never crouch down or turn your back to retrieve said objects.
8. Fight back and try to remain standing if you are attacked.

Trail *Violence*

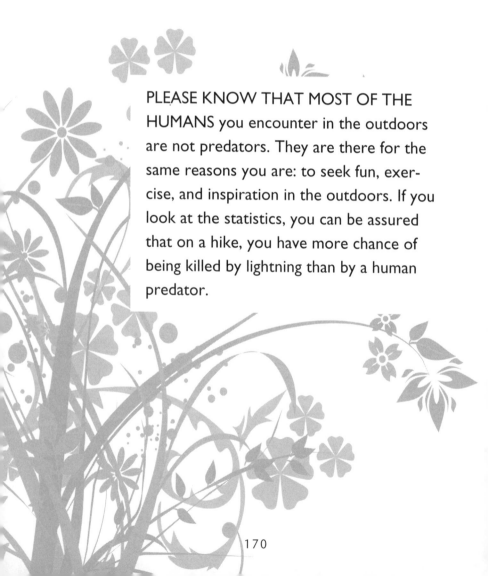

PLEASE KNOW THAT MOST OF THE HUMANS you encounter in the outdoors are not predators. They are there for the same reasons you are: to seek fun, exercise, and inspiration in the outdoors. If you look at the statistics, you can be assured that on a hike, you have more chance of being killed by lightning than by a human predator.

Still, sadly, there are trail risks of the human variety. Know from the get-go that your largest concern regarding crimes in the outdoors will be theft from your car at a trailhead—so never leave valuables in your car. Leave them at home. (If you do have any "attractables," lock them in your car's trunk.)

What other crimes can happen in the outdoors? Well, the media report chilling stories of women being attacked, raped, or killed in the outdoors by men. With luck, your biggest irritant when hiking with a man—whether he's your boyfriend, husband, dad, friend, or a passerby—will be how loudly he chews his granola bar. Are men hairy beasts, attacking women on hikes at random, at all hours of the day, every day of the week, all the time? The answer is no. That said, it's important to be aware when you're on the trail.

Some hiking reference material recommends that all women pack a gun when they are hiking by themselves. What's wrong with this safety tip? It's the "hiking by them-selves" that is a red flag. The absolute best thing that you can do to protect yourself is to never, never, never hike by yourself. Packing heat is not the best solution.

While I was writing this book, a woman was kidnapped on a holiday hike in the north Georgia mountains. She was killed three days later and found decapitated. An experienced outdoorswoman and an expert in martial arts, she was also hiking with her dog, which was later recovered alive. The man who led authorities to her body has pleaded guilty to her murder and is serving a life sentence. He has also been indicted in Florida for the murder of a woman whose body was found in a national forest, and he's suspected in the murders of an elderly couple hiking in North Carolina. These are horrible, unfortunate incidents, but in no way common occurrences. Do not let them deter you from having an out-doors life, or any life for that matter.

Hunting Season

Check with local authorities if you're unsure of the current hunting situation in your hiking area, and dress in bright clothing. Always dress your dog in blaze orange when you are hiking near hunters. We have a special doggie vest for our 60-pound pup, whose coloring and size could easily be mistaken for those of a small deer.

Of all the things that women need to buffer themselves against, rape seems to be at the top of the list. Rape is not just a physical assault, but an act of violence that leaves heavy emotional scars. According to the U.S. Department of Justice, a staggering 33 percent of women are likely to be raped in the United States in all types of locations. What is most shocking is that 80 percent of these crimes are committed by someone the woman knows. With all of that in mind, here are precautions to help you prevent an attack on the trail:

• Never, never, never hike by yourself. (Have I said that before?)

• Never separate from your hiking buddy. Establish an alarm or signal system to be used in distress. (Remember your whistle from your Hiker's Dozen!)

• Be sure that you know the person you are hiking with—particularly if that person is a man. Never go out on the trail with someone that you just met, especially in a "first date" scenario. (In the California anecdote about the woman carrying the sharpened yellow pencils, on page 82, the story is amusing in the retelling, but the woman was extremely lucky.)

• Talk to rangers and other officials to determine if there are any compromised areas you should avoid.

• At the trailhead, be cautious. When you are ready to leave, have your key in your hand, don't waste time, get in your car as soon as you open the door, and lock it. If no one is around, you may take a moment to refresh yourself, as described in the "Bathroom Breaks" section. If anything looks suspicious, drive away immediately.

• If you suspect someone, or have had a risky encounter on the trail, report it to law enforcement authorities immediately.

First Aid

BEING PREPARED ON YOUR HIKE for any circumstance is key to a lifetime of successful and safe experiences on the trail. If, in your heart of hearts, you want to do some serious trekking, then take a basic or refresher first-aid class to boost your confidence on the trails. If you want to be even more prepared, look for a wilderness- or outdoor-focused first-aid class or program.

Before heading out on any hike, familiarize yourself with area safety precautions, vital phone numbers, and, if applicable, the location of ranger stations. And, of course, always tell someone where you will be going and when you will return. (I will continue to nag about this!)

You may also consider connecting with a search-and-rescue resource, such as the one we have in Colorado (CORSAR; see page 184). If you need to be rescued, this type of program can save your life and lessen the cost of your emergency.

Most likely you will never have to deal with severe accidents or rescue situations, but you may encounter common problems that require first-aid treatment. You will, of course, be prepared, because you have your handy-dandy first-aid kit in your Hiker's Dozen essentials (see page 56)!

Cuts, scrapes, blisters, and sunburn are the typical medical attention-getters on the trail. Waiting until you get home to treat such conditions, if they are not too uncomfortable, is just fine. But if they need immediate attention, it just takes a few minutes and a few items from your kit to get you back on the trail. Other injuries or illnesses require you to do the best you can for yourself or your hiking buddy (see some basics below), until you can get professional medical help.

MINOR CUTS AND SCRAPES: Simply wash out the wound with clean water from your water bottle and bandage it up. You can clean it with antiseptic or soap and re-bandage it when you get home. For deeper cuts, wash with clean water and stop the bleeding by pressing directly onto the wound. Apply a butterfly bandage to keep the cut closed—with the thin part of the bandage covering the wound.

BLISTERS: Cover the swollen skin with a bandage or moleskin, and be on your way. Do not pop the blister, as this will add to your discomfort and subject the blister to infection.

SUNBURN: The best treatment is *pretreatment*. Apply sunscreen at least 30 minutes to an hour before you go outside (wear sunscreen underneath your clothing, as sun can penetrate thin layers of fabric), and then frequently reapply to exposed areas during your hike. Also consider some SPF lip balm for sensitive lips, and an opaque sun block containing zinc oxide for noses and lips. Wear a hat and sunglasses, and, if you are even more diligent, invest in some of the clothing designed to block ultraviolet rays (see "Go Shopping!" in Part Two of this book).

If you find yourself sunburned at the end of the day, cool the skin with aloe vera or lotion. For particularly harsh sunburns, you may also need to soothe the skin with cool wet cloths and perhaps cortisone lotions. Headache, fever, chills, and nausea can sometime accompany bad sunburn, so treat the symptoms accordingly.

SPRAINED ANKLE: Unfortunately a common injury among hikers, this turn of events, so to speak, will certainly end the day on the trail. A sprained ankle is when the ligaments are damaged after a twist or fall. The pain involved with a sprain is usually on the outer side of the ankle below the bone that bulges out. Although it is painful, an ankle sprain is usually not completely immobilizing, and it's not likely to strand you in the wilderness.

The first thing you need to do with a sprain is cool the area and compress it. An ice pack placed in a bandage and wrapped over your ankle works best, but unless you are near snow or a cold stream, this may not be an option. So, on to the first-aid kit in your pack: Place some padding on the sore area for pressure, then use your bandage material to wrap the ankle, starting at the toes and working your way up. After the ankle is wrapped, elevate the leg as soon as you can to minimize swelling. Seek medical attention as soon as possible.

FRACTURES: If you've fractured a bone or torn a joint, you will need to fashion a splint. (In basic terms, splinting involves binding something hard and solid to the broken bone.) If you suspect the bone is broken, assume it is and treat it as such: it is always smart to err on the side of caution. A broken bone can be painful and is usually accompanied by swelling and bruising. Unless there is immediate danger, a person with a fracture should not be moved until the bone has been splinted properly. Splinting prevents motion and usually keeps the bone from further damaging surrounding tissue.

For suspected arm or shoulder fractures, you can usually splint the injury by placing the forearm in a sling across the lower body and binding the arm and sling to the body. You can create a sling out of bandage material in your day pack's first-aid kit; you also can rig one up from an item of clothing, such as a belt or long neck scarf.

For a broken leg, if materials are not available to make such a splint, you can always splint one leg to the other by binding them together.

For fractures causing a bone to protrude from the skin, or causing severe deformities, try to maneuver the bone back to its natural state as best you can. No need to clean the area thoroughly at this point; just make sure debris is out of the wound. Get medical attention as soon as you can.

POISON IVY, OAK, AND SUMAC: Recognizing these three villains and avoiding contact with them is the most effective way to prevent the painful, itchy rashes they cause in many people. In most areas, poison ivy ranges from a thick, tree-hugging vine to a shaded ground cover, three leaflets to a leaf. Poison oak occurs as either a vine or shrub, with three leaflets as well (hence "leaves of three, let them be"). Poison sumac flourishes in swampland, each leaf containing 7 to 13 leaflets. Urushiol, the oil in the sap of these plants, is responsible for the rash.

Creative Splinting

To make a splint, you can use wood, branches or, in camping situations, your sleeping pad. In addition to bandages from your first-aid kit, you can use a bandanna or other extra clothing to wrap the splint.

Usually within 12 to 14 hours of exposure (but sometimes much later), raised lines and/or blisters will appear, accompanied by a terrible itch. Refrain from scratching, because bacteria under fingernails can cause infection. Wash and dry the affected area thoroughly, applying calamine lotion or another product to help dry out the rash further. If itching or blistering is severe, seek medical attention. Remember that oil-contaminated clothes, pets, or hiking gear can easily cause an irritating rash on you or someone else, so wash not only any exposed parts of your body but also your clothing, gear, pets, and anything else you or said items touch.

ALTITUDE SICKNESS: Nothing ruins an outing more often than the body's resistance to higher-than-accustomed-to altitudes. The illness is usually characterized by vomiting, loss of breath, extreme headache, lightheadedness, sleeplessness, and an overall sick feeling. Our advice: take it easy. When traveling to a higher altitude, give your body a day or two to adjust to less oxygen, hotter sun, and less air pressure than you are used to. Drink plenty of water, and lay off the alcohol and cigarettes. Wear sunglasses and sunscreen. It's that easy. As always, if serious symptoms persist, locate the nearest emergency room or call 911.

HEAT EXHAUSTION: Heat exhaustion occurs after prolonged exposure to high temperatures and high humidity. Coupled with low water consumption and excessive perspiration, it can lead to nausea and possibly fainting. It is not as severe as heatstroke (see below), and the symptoms are very different:

1. Body temperature is normal.

2. Skin is white, pale, and clammy.

3. Victim is weak, nauseated, dizzy.

4. Victim has severe cramps.

5. Victim may faint.

To treat heat exhaustion, move to a cool, shaded area. Drink water; even sips of saltwater help unless there is vomiting. Lay the victim down and raise her feet; loosen clothing and do anything to get her cool. If symptoms worsen, become severe, or last longer than one hour, get medical attention.

HEATSTROKE: Extremely high body temperature is a life-threatening emergency and you must act quickly to get the victim's body temperature down. Keep a thermometer in your pack if you hike a lot in the summer, or in warmer climates, and know the symptoms of this dire situation:

1. Any body temperature above 103°F is alarming and should be treated immediately.

2. Skin is hot, red, and dry.

3. Pulse is rapid and strong.

4. Victim may become unconscious.

Get medical assistance as soon as possible. Meanwhile, protect the victim from the sun, and undress her and sponge the bare skin with cool water from your water bottle or a nearby stream, if possible. Apply cold packs if you have them.

Once indoors, place the victim in a tub of cold water, but not with ice. Continue this treatment until the body temperature lowers or medical help arrives and takes over.

HYPOTHERMIA: Hypothermia occurs when your core body temperature is dangerously low. Cold temperatures, wind, rain, and snow set the stage for this affliction, but this condition can occur at any time of the year. Even when temperatures are far from freezing, hypothermia may result from a combination of moisture, wind chill, cool breezes, and drizzle. "Wet is not warm" is the slogan reminding you to keep your inside layer as dry as possible to prevent hypothermia. Thus the need to dress in layers that wick chilling perspiration and that maintain stable body temperature. (See "Go Shopping!" in Part Two of this book.)

Know the symptoms so you can diagnose hypothermia before it progresses along the list below:

1. Uncontrolled shivering; feet and hands are cold.

2. Loss of dexterity; clumsiness.

3. Short-term memory loss.

4. Shaking; muscles are rigid.

5. Collapse.

Treat the symptoms as soon as possible with heat, warm air, or "buddy warming"—huddling with several people, holding each other closely to preserve body heat. Ditch any wet clothing, which means wearing dry clothes, a sleeping bag, nothing at all, or some combination of these. This is not a time to be modest!

FROSTBITE: This is a close cousin to hypothermia and is usually not as deadly. However, the loss of appendages can be devastating. Direct exposure to cold causes frostbite, which is quite simply the freezing of a body part. Frostbite occurs when ice crystals form in the fluid of the cells of skin and tissues. The cheeks, nose, ears, toes, and fingers are most at risk. Like hypothermia, frostbite is a progression into something serious, as these symptoms reveal:

1. Look for skin that is flushed or red.

2. Continue to monitor skin that becomes gray or white.

3. Take note of extreme pain that then subsides.

4. The affected area becomes numb and extremely cold.

Note: *Others often notice symptoms of frostbite in a companion before that person is aware of it.*

To treat the symptoms, cover the frozen area as soon as possible, and protect it from further injury. Never walk, or let anyone else walk, on frozen feet. If fingers or toes are involved, put sterile gauze between them to keep them separated. Warm the frostbitten area rapidly but gently, as frostbitten tissue is easily damaged. *Do not rub it.* Use warm water, not hot water. If you don't have water, gently wrap the frostbitten area in warm fabric of any sort. Be sure to discontinue warming when the part becomes red. Stimulate the frostbitten area with gentle movement and keep it raised. Keep calm and hydrated until you can get help or can get indoors.

Once indoors, clean the frostbitten area with water and mild soap and make it as sterile as possible. Never rub the frozen part, or pop blisters. Never sit near a fire, stove, or heat source. Don't use heat lamps, hot water bottles, electric blankets, or heating pads.

LIFESAVING: In a medical emergency, you should follow three general stages. The following text does not take the place of first-aid training, but it is intended as a useful reminder of the procedures you would need to be aware of in case of a life-and-death situation on the trail.

1. STAGE ONE: *check for breathing and administer CPR if necessary.* Never move an injured person unless you need to do so to get them out of danger. There are exceptions due to certain perils. A drowning victim must be pulled from the water, of course, and someone close to falling rocks or an avalanche would have to be moved. Otherwise, first establish that she is breathing. Try to feel her breath on your hand, listen for exhalation, or watch the rise and fall of her chest.

If you can't determine breathing, make sure there is no airway blockage. If there is a blockage, try to fish out the object with your finger or attempt the Heimlich maneuver if you are trained to do so.

If you determine she is not breathing, start breathing for her by administering the pulmonary part of CPR (cardiopulmonary resuscitation): Cover the victim's nostrils with your hand and place your mouth directly onto her mouth and breathe deeply. Watch her chest rise, then let her exhale. Do this one time every five seconds for adults and one time every three seconds for children. If the victim has a pulse, but still does not breathe, you will need to continue this procedure until rescue arrives. If she is not breathing and does not have a pulse, you will need to administer full CPR by adding chest compressions between breaths.

In cases of massive, life-threatening bleeding, apply firm pressure directly to the wound for at least 10 to 15 minutes to allow clotting to take place and to prevent further bleeding. If a person's limb is bleeding, lift the arm or leg above the heart level.

2. STAGE TWO: *stabilize the victim and prevent shock.* After the initial critical emergency, make the hiker comfortable,

stable, and check for further injuries. The most important danger to watch for at this point is shock, but you should treat the victim for shock whether or not she is showing the symptoms. Shock victims usually appear pale and have cool, clammy skin. They may be dizzy and even faint or black out. The heartbeat is very rapid, and breathing will be quick. The victim may be nauseated and thirsty and show signs of severe anxiety. People can die from shock, and this happens when the blood pressure plummets and drops near zero.

To treat shock, lay the victim flat and loosen her clothing. Her body temperature will not be able to regulate itself, so you will need to warm or cool her accordingly. If there is no head, neck, or torso injury, elevate her legs about ten inches. Try to keep her talking and awake and assess if there are any additional injuries. While you decide what to do next, monitor her condition and vital signs, and keep talking to her. At this stage you will be simply stabilizing and preventing further injury.

3. STAGE THREE: *get the injured party out of the wilderness and into the care of rescue or medical authorities.* If she can't move on her own, either carry her out (an option if several people are in your hiking group) or send someone in your group to get help. You can also flag down fellow hikers to get help for you, or try to signal authorities that you are in trouble. (Here's where your cell phone is a lifesaver, if you have reception in your location.) Sometimes accident victims can walk out on their own, but make sure to assess that no further injuries will result, and have them walk slowly, with several resting breaks.

Wild-animal Attack

First aid for this situation follows the same basic lifesaving sequence described in this section: maintain breathing, protect against shock, and seek help. Even a seemingly minor animal bite can result in infection, tetanus, or rabies. A tetanus immunization shot, plus a booster every ten years, keeps you protected against tetanus from puncture wounds. Immunization against rabies is also available, and the immunization can be given within 48 hours of injury.

Lost!

BEING LOST IN THE WILDERNESS— or just having a momentary inkling that you *may* be lost—can be terrifying.

Search and Rescue

Check where you live or at your destination to see about the availability of emergency-rescue assistance. We don't leave home without our membership card for CORSAR (Colorado Outdoor Recreation Search and Rescue). At most Colorado outdoors shops, such as REI, you can buy a one-year card for $3 or spend $12 and buy a five-year card. CORSAR is not insurance—it does not pay for all medical transportation, which may include helicopter flights or ground ambulance. The card does allow reimbursement to county sheriffs for costs included on a mission. These expenses can include mileage, meals, equipment, gasoline, and rental fees for transport (horses, ATVs, aircraft) used in the search. It says right on the CORSAR information that "you have helped ensure that trained and well-equipped search and rescue teams will respond should you become lost or in need of rescue, and they will not have to incur undue expense due to your emergency."

SO LET'S *PLAN* FOR STAYING FOUND:

- Keep your day pack stocked with the Hiker's Dozen essentials, which include staying-found items such as your map, cell phone, whistle, compass, and GPS. (And be sure you know how to use your compass and/or GPS.)
- Always tell someone where you are going. Call them, e-mail them, talk to them. (I think I have now said this more times than I've mentioned chocolate in this book!)
- Never go hiking alone. Remember the buddy system.

ACT ON STAYING FOUND:

- Stay on designated trails. Most hikers get disoriented when they leave the path. Even on the most clearly marked trails, there is usually a point where you have to stop and consider which direction to head.
- Always remain alert and observant. Along your trail, note unique landmarks such as boulders or trees or particular vistas. Commit them to memory.
- Listen for noises such as traffic, water, or animals. Remember where you heard them.
- Arrange an alert system with your buddy, in case you get separated. ("We'll blow our whistles for three rounds of three blows," you could agree, for example.)

DON'T PANIC:

- As soon as you think you may be off-track, stop walking.
- Determine your last known location on your map, then retrace your steps to the point where you went awry. Using map, compass, and/or GPS, reorient yourself.
- If you are still not getting where you want to be, watch for passersby and ask for directions back to the trailhead or to a point on your map that reassures you.

GET YOURSELF FOUND:

- If you are truly lost, sit down, conserve all energy and supplies, and relax.
- Don't leave the area.
- Listen for sounds, and make a noise if you hear something.
- Attract attention in any way possible: Blow your whistle at varying intervals; tie a piece of cloth (your scarf or bandanna) on a high branch; flash anything in your pack that is reflective (a mirror, aluminum foil); light a signal fire; draw or place rocks onto the ground in a large pattern.

- Find shelter, and keep as warm, dry, or cool as possible. If you are in a remote area and haven't seen a human for hours, a smoky fire is a sure way to get the attention of local authorities. This is where the matches in your day pack come in handy. Of course, make sure you start a controlled fire; you don't want to start a forest fire. Typically, multiple fires set within a triangle signal that there is trouble. Also, if you are trying to send ground-to-air symbols, arrange your gear in a large vertical line to signal help is needed.

I can remember walking as a child. It was not customary to say you were fatigued. It was customary to complete the goal of the expedition.

—*Katharine Hepburn*

PART SEVEN

AFTER
SUNDOWN

Camping
101

IN THE "FIT HIKING" SECTION (PART FOUR), I commented on the difference between a single outing for a few hours, and long hikes over consecutive days. You need more stamina and endurance and wind power. However, I also noted that the rewards multiply, as well.

So now that you have come to love hiking and have acquired all of these outdoor skills, it may be time to move on to backpacking and overnight adventures. Probably like you, I relish my share of hotel rooms and fancy resorts. But overnighting in nature is my favorite way to see the world.

Once again, one of the first things you may need to do is to go shopping. Yeah! Unless your family already has equipment, you'll need to rent, borrow, or purchase overnight shelter (that is, a tent) and a bed (a sleeping bag). As you trek through this section, you may also see other needs, such as some camp cooking equipment.

Let's assume you're interested in buying, or will be someday, and I'll pass on some tips from my trials and errors.

In these pages, I'll also walk you through what to expect in arranging for a campsite, setting up your "bedroom," and generally preparing yourself for this extraordinary opportunity to spend more time in nature.

ON YOUR BACK—the Pack

Your day pack won't have enough room for the supplies you will need for a journey of one or more nights. Some manufacturers offer backpack styles that take into account the shape and size of a woman to make the perfect fit. But, generically speaking, you'll have a choice of those with external frames and those with internal frames.

The external-frame backpack has an aluminum frame that the backpack is attached to. Although the external frame packs are more old school than the internal ones, they still have hard-core supporters. These packs are usually comfortable, have a lot of compartments that are easy to find, provide a nice space between your back and the pack, and cost less.

Internal-frame packs have the frame built into the pack and are what you will typically see today on the average backpacker traveling through Europe or camping locally. Internal frame packs fit closer to your back and can be adjusted with various straps and closures to fit your body. This closer fit gives more stability and comfort and flexes with your body as you move.

The TENT

Unless you plan to sleep under the stars on your overnight camping trip, you will need this portable roof over your head. There are many types of tents from countless manufacturers, so finding a tent should be an easy and enjoyable process. Something is out there for everyone!

Freestanding tents are the most popular. You can camp on any surface and, unless it is windy, you will not need to stake down the tent. Most backpacking tents are made of nylon and polyester, or a blend of both, with sections of mesh and almost always a waterproof floor. Some are made with a waterproof outer region, but most likely they are not, so it is best to invest in a *rainfly*. That is a detachable piece of material that drapes over the framework of the tent to prevent rain from permeating the tent walls.

If you are truly backpacking, you're hauling your tent around on your back, with all of your camping necessities. (Of course, with a tent large enough for you and at least one other buddy, one of you won't be dealing with the tent weight.) But still, size and weight will be critical considerations in your tent purchase. The most-common type for backpackers is the three-season tent, perfect for almost all weather except bitterly cold winter conditions and extremely high winds. For carrying comfort, your tent should weigh around five to seven pounds.

You will note some rather contradictory-sounding requirements that a good tent has to fulfill: It should be lightweight and easy to set up, but also durable. It should have plenty of ventilation but also be easily zipped up to keep out cold and wind. If you tend to hike in warm or tropical climates, make sure you get one with mosquito-protective netting, as well. (For example, REI offers a Bug Hut 2 tent that sleeps two under a veil of insect-prohibiting mesh.)

The ground is hard, cold, and uncomfortable, so the most important part of your bed-in-the-wilderness is your sleeping bag—and whether or not to use a ground pad or ground cloth (see below). Sleeping bags, like tents, come in varying weights and sizes, but the most popular and versatile choice for backpackers is the three-season version. As the name implies, this type of bag is usable for spring, summer, and fall conditions (above 20°F), and weighs between three and four pounds, depending on the filler used.

If you are hiking and camping in colder months, you will need to get a winter bag designed for conditions of 0°F and below. If you know you will be sleeping in warmer weather (remember most hiking locations cool down in the evening), a summer or ultralight bag is ideal, not only because you won't melt inside your sleeping bag, but also because it is considerably lighter to carry.

When you buy your sleeping bag, consider these features:

- Shape of the bag (mummy, semirectangular, rectangular)
- Quality of the stitching
- Zipper placement
- Fabric
- Filler
- Size

Most sleeping bags come in short, regular, and tall. Decide if you want a hood, extra pockets, and other features. And, of course, make sure you are comfortable and happy with the materials. If you are allergic to down, buy a bag with synthetic filler. The shell of the sleeping bag should be made of a material that is comfortable and feels nice next to your skin.

GROUND CLOTH OR PAD: A ground cloth helps keep your sleeping bag clean, and it doesn't add much bulk to your pack. But if you have room, consider a pad as well, to slip between the ground cloth and your sleeping bag. A pad both cushions and insulates. There are two major types: a simple foam pad or an inflating pad. When deciding on which type to buy, think of the weight and bulk you are willing to carry. A thin foam pad may not be the most glamorous choice, but your fellow hikers may envy you when they realize how much lighter your pack is.

PRACTICE PITCH: Pitching a tent in your backyard and spending a night under the stars is a great way to get ready for sleeping away from home in the outdoors. But it's nothing like the thrill of carrying your tent in your pack and then bedding down for the night in a pristine campsite. There is more to it than just plopping down in any beautiful spot, however, and the next section helps get you on the right track to that scenic site.

RESERVATIONS *and* PERMITS

Many backcountry sites require that you reserve your site ahead of time. Obtain all permits and authorization as required; check in, pay your fee; and mark your site as directed. Don't make the mistake of grabbing a seemingly empty site that looks more appealing than your site. It could be reserved. Even in the backcountry. You don't want to find out in the middle of the night.

To minimize the impact of camping in regional, state, and national parks, regulations typically limit the number of permits issued. You may obtain day-of-trip permits for some backcountry sites, but I recommend making your reservation by mail, Internet, or in person as soon as you know when and where you want to go. Some popular backcountry sites near me open up for reservations for the summer season as early as the prior October.

Rocky Mountain National Park (RMNP) is in my back-yard, figuratively speaking, and it has a backcountry-campsite system that is organized to a *T*. I want to use their regulations to walk you through what you may encounter as you plan a backpacking adventure.

You must have a backcountry permit to camp overnight in RMNP's backcountry. You may pick one up at the Headquarters Backcountry Office or another visitor center. For all reservations, you must give them your vitals and list an itinerary with dates that correspond to campsites where you plan to stay. I always check on the snowpack for some of the campsites, as there is still snow in RMNP in the summer. You have to tell them how many people will be in your party. There is a limit of seven per party for *individual* campsites and a limit of 12 per party for *group* campsites.

For each permit in RMNP, you'll pay a $20 administrative fee when the permit is actually issued. A Backcountry Trip Planning Worksheet is available online and they encourage you to have it filled out and handy when you make an in-person or phone reservation. During the winter and early spring, when the backcountry is not used as frequently, you can self-register; but come summer, you must pick up the permit by 10 a.m. on the first day of your planned backcountry stay. Otherwise the permit is cancelled in its entirety and given to other backpackers.

Your permit is considered a contract between you and the National Park Service, and you must agree that:

- You will treat the backcountry with respect; and

- You will take care of the wilderness.

Each permit lists the park regulations on the back and you
must read, understand, sign, and obey them. The permit is
then attached, in plain view, on the outside of your backpack.
When you reach your camp, you attach the permit to the
outside of your tent. The permit indicates the number of
people in your party and specifies the campsite for each night
you are in the park.

During RMNP's busiest months, June to September,
campers may stay in the backcountry for three consecutive
nights in one camp area. Between October and May, campers may stay in the backcountry for a maximum of 14 nights
with no more than a total of 21 nights per year. RMNP also
prefers small clusters of campers, because fewer people per
site imposes less impact on the park's fragile resources.

Therefore, for *individual* campsites, RMNP allows from one
to seven people, and each camping area has one to six sites.
Groups, considered to be 8 to 12 people, may not spread
themselves over neighboring individual sites, but must split up
and camp at least 1 mile apart, or else use *group* sites, intended
for more people. I cite these details because this is the type
of requirement you will encounter in many state and national
parks. It is all for the protection of these beautiful places.

If you end a trip early, you must notify an RNMP ranger
to cancel the permit, so other backpackers may take your
place. You also are asked to report all unusual wildlife sightings, trail conditions, or incidents to a ranger. If you see any
violations of rules and regulations, you should report them to
a ranger as soon as possible.

CAMPSITE

On a backpacking trip, it's a good idea to establish a base
camp instead of moving camp every day. This way you can set
out each day from the same place for different hikes.

When requesting a site, or when you are being booked into a site, here is a reasonable wish list:

- Access to breathtaking scenery and points of interest in the general area
- Some degree of privacy; many sites are grouped together, so you may have company nearby
- Green space, with shrubs and trees between adjoining sites, as well as staggered sites (for example, the entrance to the site across the way is not directly opposite yours)

Some backcountry sites are surprisingly large; others are incredibly small. Many of my favorites are influenced to a great extent by the quiet. How far away can you get from the fray? You can usually expect some variation of privacy, space, and unfettered scenery depending on whether you visit a backcountry site during the week, on a weekend, or on a holiday.

SECURITY: I find that most backcountry sites are very safe and secure. This is due largely to the presence of park rangers controlling backcountry permits and then making their rounds. The only places that might be compromised are those extremely remote backcountry sites that are not regulated, have few visitors, and have no ranger district.

CLEANLINESS: This should be a no-brainer, since you are in the backcountry. If you can tell someone has been there, it's not clean. Trash, tent stakes, and burnt logs are a real turnoff.

SETTLING IN: Pitch your tent in a designated area, and on a level surface. A "bed" of leaves, pine straw, or grass is ideal, but don't put your tent on undisturbed vegetation. Never dig a trench around your tent.

And don't forget to look up! Recall my story in this book's "Wicked Weather and Natural Hazards" section: A hiker was felled by and died because of a falling limb. *Do not set up your tent under a tree or limb that looks loose or broken.*

The Art of Building a Fire

Here's a quick review, in case you haven't done this for a while—a fire needs three basic elements: fuel (wood), heat (or flame), and air (or oxygen). When building wood fires, different sizes of wood are needed: tinder, kindling, and larger wood, called the fuel.

❏ TINDER is the fire starter and is small, dry material that burns immediately. It can be wood, pine needles, leaves, pinecones, or dead bark.

❏ KINDLING can be twigs, sticks, or small pieces of wood and bark, but it must be large enough to ignite larger fuel, or wood, and thin and dry enough to burn quickly.

❏ FUEL is the larger wood that keeps the fire going. It also should be dry. Fuel can be logs, or pieces of wood or bark either found in the area or brought in with you. Make sure to check local rules to see if wood-gathering is allowed in your location.

❏ HARDWOODS (such as maple, oak, hickory, and birch) provide longer-burning fires than softwoods (such as pine, aspen, cedar, or spruce). However, softwoods provide great initial fuel for a fire maintained by hardwoods.

Also do a little site maintenance, such as picking up small rocks and sticks that can damage your tent floor and make sleep uncomfortable. If you have a separate tent rainfly, but don't need it, keep it rolled up at the base of the tent in case it starts to rain. You can also use it underneath your tent to thwart ground moisture and protect the tent floor.

☐ GET 'ER STARTED: Find a place to build the fire, such as an existing fire pit or ring, or clear a space on the ground and dig a small pit. Make a small triangle with three sticks or pieces of kindling. Place a layer of tinder upright in the middle of the triangle against the top stick. Arrange a layer of kindling on top of the layer of tinder in a cone or tepee formation and leave an opening so you have space to light the tinder.

Keep reserves of kindling and tinder nearby to add to the fire as it takes hold. Using a match or lighter, ignite the tinder and gently fan it until it lights the surrounding kindling. Once the kindling is strongly burning, add the main fuel logs and pieces of wood carefully so that you feed the fire rather than extinguish it. Continue to stoke the fire with kindling and fuel.

When you are ready to let the fire die down, let it burn until only ashes remain. Stir the ashes and add water; repeat until no gray ash is left. You can also use sand to extinguish a fire. Before you leave the area, make sure the fire is completely cold and *out*. Check and double-check again. Cover the fire area with sand, dirt, and rocks to return the area to its natural condition.

CAMPFIRE

Before you set out on your backpacking venture, look into the park or area's rules regarding fire building. Are fires allowed? How will a fire impact that environment? Has the area been unseasonably hot, windy, or affected by a drought?

Know this before you load up your pack, because you may have to bring a backpackers' camp stove.

If you are allowed to build a fire, choose a spot a safe distance from trails, tents, and low-hanging branches or flammable ground cover. Make sure you also have water or sand nearby to quickly extinguish fires if needed. Never burn your camping trash. Trash smoke smells horrible and trash debris in a fire pit is hard to pack out.

WATER

Some hikers and backpackers hit the trail prepared to purify water found along the route. This method, while less dangerous than drinking it untreated, comes with risks. Purifiers with ceramic filters are the safest. Many hikers pack along the slightly distasteful tetraglycine–hydroperiodide tablets to debug water (sold under the names Potable Aqua, Coughlan's, and others). Or boil water at your campsite for a minimum of ten minutes.

However you decide to deal with water, this is another friendly reminder from me that you will need a lot of it for a two- to three-day backpacking expedition. You'll need it not only for preventing your own dehydration but also for cooking, cleanup, and grooming.

For nondrinking water, you can use water from a nearby stream or lake, but be sure to carry it at least 70 adult steps, or 200 feet, from the water source to wash yourself or your dishes. Never wash directly in a lake or stream, and be sure to use biodegradable soap.

FOOD

When hiking with your buddies, make sure that it is understood who eats what, who cooks what, when you will eat it, and who cleans up. Nothing causes group dynamics to curdle faster than miscommunication about food.

At RMNP, as at many parks, you have to cook meals with a portable stove because fires are not allowed. Especially with so many wildfires raging these past few years, there is just too much potential for cooking fires to get out of control if they aren't well tended. Be sure you know how to use your stove and its fuel source—and how to repair your stove—before you go backpacking the first time. Cook a couple of meals at home on the stove so you are familiar with it.

When you choose the food to take, think about the logistics involved in preparation. Try to pick foods that will need minimal cookware and minimal cleanup. At home, keep "camp" foods—dry goods such as pasta and rice, fixings for a simple dinner and breakfast, bulk cocoa and nuts, and per-ishables such as cheese—on hand so you can go backpacking on short notice. For convenience, and to avoid waste, pack-age camp foods into plastic bags in the estimated amounts that you will need for every meal on the expedition. Don't take along bulky boxes or cans if you can avoid it.

Some backpackers buy items such as peanut butter and jelly in handy squeeze tubes. A very popular backpacking enterprise is freeze-dried food. While I am not a fan, the major benefit of freeze-dried food is convenience. I prefer to pack the extra weight and have a yummy entrée and dessert. Freeze-drying preserves food by removing water, making it safe from attack by microorganisms. Many of the meals require you to just add boiling water. The downsides of these foods are taste, texture, and expense.

Other backpacking enterprises to look into if you really get into the scene include: MREs (Meals Ready to Eat); back-country baking; freeze-drying your own food; mixing your own GORP (see recipe for Good Old Raisins and Peanuts

Kim's Camp Cuisine

GORP (Good Old Raisins and Peanuts): Fill plastic snack bags chock-full of almonds, peanuts, butterscotch chips, dark-chocolate chips, and raisins. Blend. Eat. Heaven. Anytime.

FOR A QUICK OVERNIGHT HIKE: Cheese and bagel sandwiches; precooked spaghetti with my favorite sauce (most likely leftover); sliced French bread or a hard roll; orange juice; oatmeal with dates and brown sugar; and coffee supplies (including the herb stevia for sweetening).

above); and making or modifying your own camp cookware. Whatever the case, it is important to know how to buy, pack, prepare, store, handle, and preserve food for a variety of hiking activities in different weather conditions.

BEARPROOFING: A metal "bear" canister for storing food and another for scented personal items (soap, deodorant, and toothpaste) is highly recommended in any camping situation. The canisters add weight and take up room, but they will provide you with the greatest security. You will have your food, and it won't get eaten up by bears and insects.

Avoid bringing or preparing greasy and smelly foods into the backcountry. Never take food into your sleeping area. It's all just too appealing to the wildlife.

CLEANUP DETAIL: Seal all food scraps and garbage in airtight containers or storage bags and carry it with you out of the backcountry. Take all uneaten food out with you, too. *Never leave food behind in the wilderness.*

When disposing of wash water, first filter out all food scraps and pack them into the garbage container. Then toss out the wash water by throwing it over a wide area. Do not scatter food scraps into a lake or stream or on the ground, and never throw food into pit toilets. Wipes are a great cleanup shortcut for your utensils. A good friend of mine told *Backpacker* magazine that he licks his bowls clean and heads on his way. Whatever works for you is fine with me.

BACK *to the* BATHROOM

In RMNP, many backcountry campsites include pit toilets. Where there is no pit toilet available, visitors are asked to follow strict bathroom-break rules. First, you must pee in rocky places that won't be damaged by animals that dig for the salts and minerals found in urine. Deer, bighorn sheep, porcupines, and other mammals can destroy campsites, clothes, boots, and camping gear in search of these substances.

Second, you must either pack out solid waste or dig a "cat hole" 6 inches deep using a small trowel. Be sure that you poop at least 70 adult steps or 200 feet from water or trails. Lastly, of course, wash your hands.

If you are prone to using the bathroom multiple times during the night, plan ahead. Keep a flashlight and any other accoutrements you may need by your tent door and know exactly where to head, for the head, in the dark.

LEAVE *No* TRACE

Remember to leave only your footprints when you depart from a backcountry campsite. Pack out all of your garbage and stuff. A side effect of sloppy campers: animals paying a visit in search of dinner. An unannounced approach, a sudden movement, or a loud noise startles most animals, and a surprised animal in your campsite can be dangerous to both you and them. Give them plenty of space—and pack out your own trash to discourage future visits.

SUMMER *Backpacking* CHECKLIST

Keep your gear organized in one place at home. A big plastic bin is good for this. Organize, clean, and repair items within a day of returning from one trip so it's prepped for the next. And remember that everything you need for backpacking has to fit on your back, so pack carefully.

THE HIKER'S DOZEN (see *page 56*)

*Includes first-aid kit

SHELTER

*Tent and rainfly

PERSONAL EQUIPMENT

Don't forget your layers, and dress appropriately for the season and temperatures where you are headed. Remember that nighttime mercury can plummet.

- Backpack
- Sleeping bag and sleeping pad or ground cloth
- Biodegradable hand soap
- Toothbrush and toothpaste
- Small towel
- Boot socks and liners
- Long pants

- Shorts (or convertible long pants)
- Light shirt or tee shirt
- Warm shirt
- Jacket or outerwear (layer clothing)
- Other clothing depending on conditions and altitude
- Appropriate undergarments (panties, a sports bra, etc.)
- Personal-hygiene items (deodorant, feminine protection)
- Flip-flops (for the campsite)
- Swimming suit (optional)
- Sewing kit (optional)

TOOLS AND SUPPLIES

- Lantern
- Trowel or small shovel for digging cat holes
- Bear canister to store food
- 50-foot rope and nylon cord
- Stuff sacks and dunk bags (nylon mesh)

COOKING EQUIPMENT

- Pots and pans (nested ones are ideal)
- Stove and fuel
- Eating utensils: cup, bowl, plate, knife, fork, spoon
- Cleaning supplies: biodegradable detergent and container, sponge, scouring pad
- Collapsible bucket or water bag

Knots 101

Knots can be useful in a variety of scenarios out in the wilderness: from pitching a tent, to hitching your boat to shore, to securing first-aid bandages, to creating a makeshift leash for your dog. Every smart hiker should know how to tie at least one type of secure knot, just in case it is needed.

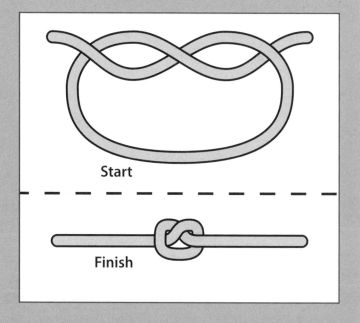

Start

Finish

❑   The most basic kind of knot is the OVERHAND KNOT. To make the knot, make a loop with your rope and bring one end around the rope and through the loop, then pull the ends of the rope tightly to secure it.

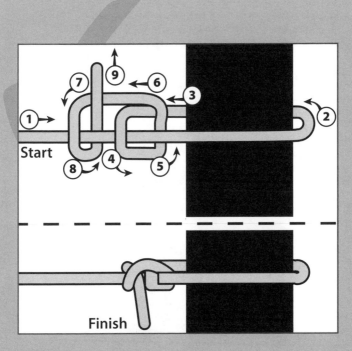

Start

Finish

❏ A HALF-HITCH KNOT is used to fasten the end of a rope after it has been looped around something, such as a tree, post, or sleeping bag. To make the knot, loop the end of the rope around the tree (or post, or sleeping bag) and make a half hitch by looping the short end of the rope under the long end and through the open space. To make it more secure, create an even more complex knot by making a second half hitch below the first half hitch. By having two half hitches, you can make a sliding knot that moves along the length of the rope. The sliding knot can be used to change the tension on the rope without your having to retie the knot each time.

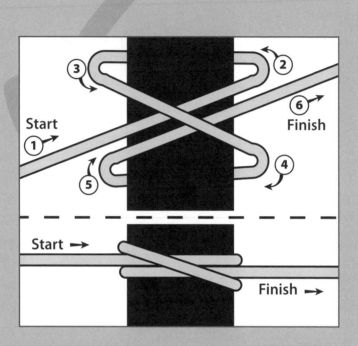

❏   A CLOVE HITCH KNOT is used to fasten one end of a rope around a tree. To make the knot, pass the short end of the rope around the back of a tree. Bring the short end around in front and cross it over the long part of the rope, making an X. Hold the X with your thumb while you wrap the rope around the tree again below the first turn. Push the rope under the X so that the end comes out between the two turns around the tree.

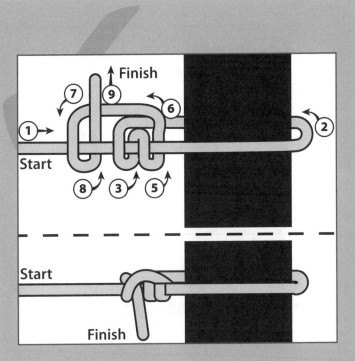

❏ A TAUT-LINE HITCH KNOT is used to make a loop that can be adjustable in length. A taut-line hitch is useful when pitching a tent and adjusting the tension on the ropes. To make the knot, loop the short end of the rope around the tent peg; wind the short end of the rope around the longer twice. Fasten the short end to the standing part with a half hitch above the previous loops. To adjust the tension of the rope, slide the knot back and forth along the rope.

❏   A BOWLINE KNOT is a loop at the end of a rope
that remains the same size and can be tied around a
waist or tree. To make the knot, make a small loop
by passing the working end over the standing end.
Bring the working end then up through the loop and
then pass it beneath the standing end of the rope,
and continue again through the loop once more.
Tighten the loop and knot by pulling on both ends of
the rope until tight.

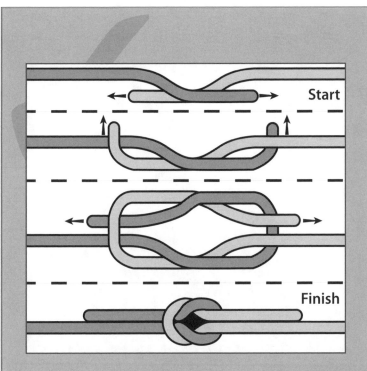

❏ A SQUARE KNOT is commonly used to tie bandages in place, or to join two ropes together. To make the knot, pass the left end of the rope over the right end; then pass the right end over the left end. Then repeat by pushing one end around and under the other and up through the formed loop. Pull tightly.

You gotta go where you wanna go,
Do what you wanna do . . .

—*The Mamas and
the Papas*

PART EIGHT

SMART &

SAVVY

Life List

Vacation
Treks

WE ALL HAVE DREAMS of where we want to go that we've never been, or what we want to do that we've never done. Sometimes I cop out when I go on vacation, and I just take a suitcase full of novels. Still, with hiking always on my mind, I do pay particular attention to the trails and outdoor adventures that different destinations offer.

After a conversation about that, my editor asked me to make a list of all the places where I love to hike. The more I thought about it, the more I wanted to encourage you, my reader, to think about where you want to go on foot. So I came up with this crazy quilt of three exercises for us.

Happy trails!
—*Kim*

EXERCISE 1: *National Parks*

The National Park Service is steward for nearly 400 natural, cultural, and recreational sites across the nation. To make your hiking-adventure wish list, I suggest that you start here. Pick a manageable number, say, six parks, and begin to plan. Since many of the parks have hundreds of miles of trails, you should have no trouble coming up with at least ten hikes per park, in that list of six, that you can complete once or even twice in your lifetime. For more information, visit **www.nps.gov.**

　FYI, here are my own six favorite national parks:

- **Glacier National Park** in Montana
- **Grand Canyon National Park** in Arizona
- **Grand Teton National Park** in Wyoming
- **Great Smoky Mountains National Park** in Tennessee
- **Rocky Mountain National Park** in Colorado
- **Yosemite National Park** in California

EXERCISE 2: *Been There, Done That, Wanna Do It Again!*

Where did you leave your heart when you traveled? (San Francisco?) Think about a place you want to see again, only this time instead of driving around in a car or sailing by in a cruise ship, you want to feel it beneath your feet, on a good long hike.

　My "gotta go again" place: the islands of Hawaii. On the Big Island, **Hawai'i Volcanoes National Park** is a land of enchantment. On this live volcano, where future islands are brewing, there are hiking trails that you will never see

Smart & Savvy Wish List:
Seven Unique Lodges and Waterways with Hiking Access

Here are the places I dream about when I'm "sleepwalking."

❏ AHWAHNEE HOTEL, YOSEMITE NATIONAL PARK, CALIFORNIA

This is one of the most distinctive and historic lodgings of all of the U.S. national parks. The Ahwahnee was specifically designed to highlight its natural surroundings, featuring Yosemite Falls, Half Dome, and Glacier Point—all world-class hiking destinations. Information: **www.yosemitepark.com.**

❏ BOUNDARY WATERS CANOE AREA, WILDERNESS, MINNESOTA

The Boundary Waters contain more than 1,200 miles of canoe routes with shoreline hiking trails and campsites. Highlights include cliffs and crags, canyons, gentle hills, rocky shores, sandy beaches, and several thousand lakes and streams, interspersed with islands and surrounded by forest. Information: **www.bwcaw.org.**

❏ BOWRON LAKE CANOE CIRCUIT, BOWRON LAKES, BRITISH COLUMBIA, CANADA

This is a unique canoe trip through the Cariboo Mountains, six major lakes, and a series of connecting streams, rivers, and portages. The canoeing is complimented by short hikes. Information: **www.bcadventure.com/adventure/ explore/cariboo/trails/bowron.htm.**

❏ EL CAPITÁN CANYON, SANTA BARBARA,
  CALIFORNIA

This eco-resort sits in a seaside pocket on
300 acres above the Southern California Pacific
coast. Access to the 2,500-acre El Capitán Canyon
is a hiker's delight. There are also surrounding
area trails and beaches for exploring. Information:
www.elcapitancanyon.com.

❏ JAS DES EYDINS, THE LUBERON VALLEY, PROVENCE,
  FRANCE

Jas des Eydins is a Provençal farmhouse inn
set amid vineyards, cherry orchards, and lavender
fields. The surrounding area is renowned for its
antique monuments, historic towns, bountiful
vineyards, picturesque hillsides—and spectacular
trails. Information: **www.jasdeseydins.com/
description/situation.htm.**

❏ LA VILLA DEL VALLE, VALLE DE GUADALUPE, MEXICO

On a hilltop in the heart of the Mexican wine
country, only 90 minutes by car from San Diego,
California, is this small luxury inn. It's a secluded
sanctuary that offers walking access to vineyards,
olive groves, mountains, and rows of lavender.
Information: **www.lavilladelvalle.com.**

❏ VOLCANO HOUSE, HAWAI'I VOLCANOES
  NATIONAL PARK, HAWAII

Nestled on the rim of the Kilauea Caldera,
the Volcano House lodge has an amazing front-
row view of an active volcano. With unparalleled
access to the park, it is a hiker's extravaganza. This
is an amazing hotel that dates back to 1846. Information: **www.volcanohousehotel.com.**

anywhere else. On Kauai, my favorite place to stay is at the **Waimea Plantation Cottages.** Beautifully restored, they sit near the base of Waimea Canyon. Again, this Hawaiian canyon is a beautiful and unique place to hike. On the north shore of Kauai, a cliffside trail with stunning Pacific views—the **Kalalau Trail**—is well worth the drive from the Waimea Canyon area. On Maui, at **Haleakala National Park,** you can experience Hawaii's most exotic natural features: hiking trails that lead to cabins and campsites that wind through jungles, past tropical flowers, with views of the ocean and Haleakala's spatter cones and lava tubes.

EXERCISE 3: *Yearly Calendar*

Create a 12-month guide to the hiking destinations of your choice. In other words, pick the time of year you want to be in a specific place to explore on foot. Or pick a faraway place *and* a close-to-home destination, as I did with October (see below). This calendar does not have to be completed in a specific calendar year, but can be pieced together over the course of many years. Do February this year, October next year, and so on.

I would put **St. Marks National Wildlife Refuge,** in St. Marks, Florida, on my list. I'd like to be on hand in one of these Octobers, when a thick swarm of migrating butterflies roosts overnight in the refuge's cedar trees; almost 50 miles of the Florida National Scenic Trail runs through this refuge, so there is lots of good hiking there. In October, I would also make sure to pay a visit to my beloved **Rocky Mountain National Park,** since prime elk bugling season is in full swing. The idea is to have someplace new and different to aspire to every month that will have you walking in new surroundings.

TRAIL MIX:
Mental Nourishment for Your Adventure

• GAUGE YOURSELF: Finding your way and becoming the person you want to be centers on your ability to read your internal position, like the fixed points on a compass or, using the GPS analogy, your internal satellites.

• BREATH OF FRESH AIR: Is it healthier inside than it is outside? NO! The U.S. Environmental Protection Agency has estimated that airborne-chemical levels in homes are as much as 70 times as high as those outside. The typical home contains more than 63 hazardous products that together contain hundreds of chemicals. The air in a typical American home is ten times more toxic than outdoors, yet Americans spend 80 to 90 percent of their time indoors.

• ABOUT THAT CELL PHONE: Your cell phone will not get you out of a jam in the backcountry! Do not ever rely on cell phones on a hiking trip. Signals and access are very inconsistent. Check with your cellular service provider before leaving home. Many outdoor enthusiasts rely on GPS (global positioning systems) and other forms of communication in the backcountry. Never make a social call on your cellular phone on a hiking trail. The noise pollution is unwarranted in the outdoors. Anything shy of an emergency can wait until you are back at the trailhead.

• BRAIN POWER: Your brain can rest in the outdoors. *Wrong.* You must take along your brain. A cool, calculating mind is the single most important piece of equipment you will ever need on the trail.

• SPEAK UP!: It isn't cool to ask for directions. Again, *wrong*. Always ask questions if you are not sure before heading out on the trail. It is a lot easier to get advice beforehand than to risk a mishap on the trail when it's too late.

• NO SURPRISES: Never spook animals. An unannounced approach, sudden movement, or loud noise startles most animals. A surprised moose can be dangerous to you, to others, and to themselves. Give animals extra room and time to adjust to your presence.

• THE SCOOP ON POOP: It's essential to pack out dog poop rather than leave it on the trail or even by the side of the trail. Dog poop is not the same as that of other animals, even that of coyotes or wolves. It's dangerous to the environment, especially near water sources, and it makes a bad impression on other hikers—not to mention their boots.

• THE SWEATY TRUTH ABOUT STINKY FEET: I read in *Backpacker* magazine that each foot has more than 125,000 sweat glands. Your best solution is to air-dry your boots and socks each night. If you have excessively sweaty feet, you have a bigger chance of getting blisters and infections. Sweat causes foot odor, ruins socks and footwear, and creates conditions for cold injuries such as frostbite and trench foot. And there's always the risk of grossing out your friends. So, what works? Dry socks; antiperspirant in a cream, roll-on, or powder; foot powder such as Gold Bond; and insoles designed to absorb sweat. If you think your condition may be serious or it seems abnormal, see a doctor.

Appendix A
Books for Your Backpack

OBVIOUSLY YOU DON'T WANT TO weigh yourself down with heavy books, but here's a list of guides and nature titles that have expanded my own hiking horizons. No matter how many miles I log on my feet, I always find for new ways to enjoy the journey—and some of my best leads lie within these pages. Many are dog-eared; some bear the telltale purple stains of a drippy PB&J sandwich enjoyed on long-ago trails, but all are treasures on my bookshelf.

THE GREAT OUTDOORS

Visit the Web site of **Menasha Ridge Press** (**www .menasharidge.com**) for a list of many titles in addition to this book that are pertinent to hiking, backpacking, and other adventures in nature.

HIKING BOOKS GEARED TOWARD WOMEN

Adventure Girl's Guide to Finding Adventure . . . Without Breaking a Nail, by Stefanie Michaels (Lulu Press, 2006)

Babes in the Woods: The Woman's Guide to Eating Well, Sleeping Well, and Having Fun in the Backcountry, by Bobbi Hoadley (Falcon, 2003)

Backpacking with Babies & Small Children, by Goldie Silverman (Wilderness Press, 1998)

Backpacking: A Woman's Guide: Everything You Need to Know to Get Started and Keep Going, by Adrienne Hall (Ragged Mountain Press, 1998)

Let's Get Primitive: The Urban Girl's Guide to Camping, by Heather Menicucci (Ten Speed Press, 2007)

Outdoor Adventures with Kids, by Mary Mapes McConnell (Taylor Publishing, 1996)

Outdoor Education in Girl Scouting (Girl Scouts of the U.S.A, 1984)

Your Own Book of Campcraft, by Catherine Hammett (Pocket Books, 1950)

HIKING BOOKS ABOUT GEAR, ESSENTIALS, AND THE OVERALL EXPERIENCE

The Ashley Book of Knots, by Clifford Ashley (Doubleday, 1944)

Backpacker: Everyday Wisdom: 1001 Expert Tips for Hikers by Karen Berger (Mountaineers Books, 1997)

Backpacker: Hiking Light Handbook, by Karen Berger (Mountaineers Books, 2004)

The Backpacker's Field Manual, by Rick Curtis (Crown Publishing, 2005)

Backpacker's Start-Up: A Beginner's Guide to Hiking & Backpacking, by Doug Werner (Tracks Publishing, 1999)

Basic Essentials: Backpacking, by Harry Roberts (Falcon, 2007)

Campfire Cuisine: Gourmet Recipes for the Great Outdoors, by Robin Donovan (Quirk Books, 2006)

Campfire Songs, by Irene Maddox (Globe Pequot, 1998)

The Complete Book of Knots, by Geoffrey Budworth (The Lyons Press, 1997)

The Creative Journal: The Art of Finding Yourself, by Lucia Capacchione (Swallow Press, 1989)

The Essential Outdoor Gear Manual, by Annie Getchell (Ragged Mountain Press, 2000)

Handbook of Nature Study, by Anna Botsford Comstock and Verne N. Rockcastle (Comstock Publishing, 1986)

Hints & Tips for Outdoor Adventure, by John Viehman (Rodale Press, 1993)

Medicine for Mountaineering (fifth edition), by James A. Wilkerson (The Mountaineers Books, 2001)

National Geographic Guide to the National Parks of the United States, by National Geographic Society (National Geographic, 2003)

National Geographic Guide to the State Parks of the United States, by National Geographic Society (National Geographic, 2004)

The Outdoors Almanac: Practical Solutions for the Wilderness Experience, by Len McDougall (Burford Books, 1999)

Walking Softly in the Wilderness: The Sierra Club Guide to Backpacking, by John Hart (Sierra Club Books, 2005)

The Whole Backpacker's Catalog: Tools and Resources for the Foot Traveler, by Edwin J. C. Sobey (Ragged Mountain Press, 1999)

Wilderness Basics, by the San Diego Chapter of the Sierra Club (Mountaineers Books, 2004)

Wilderness First Aid Manual, by William W. Forgey (HART Health and Safety, 1999)

Appendix B
World Wide Web Trail Map

CONSERVATION AND WILDERNESS ORGANIZATIONS

AMERICAN HIKING SOCIETY Advocacy group for hikers and hiking trails: **www.americanhiking.org**

AMERICAN TRAILS Sponsored group for hikers and trail users: **www.americantrails.org**

LEAVE NO TRACE CENTER FOR OUTDOOR ETHICS Public and private partnership promoting Leave No Trace practices: **www.lnt.org**

NATIONAL AUDUBON SOCIETY Environmental action with focus on birding habitat: **www.audubon.org**

NATIONAL WILDLIFE FEDERATION **www.nwf.org**

THE NATURE CONSERVANCY An organization that preserves land by buying it: **www.nature.org**

SIERRA CLUB Environmental powerhouse:
www.sierraclub.org

TREAD LIGHTLY Nonprofit emphasizing outdoor ethics:
www.treadlightly.org

THE WILDERNESS SOCIETY Wilderness advocacy with scientific
focus: **www.wilderness.org**

WORLD WILDLIFE FEDERATION **www.worldwildlife.org**

U.S. FEDERAL AND STATE AGENCIES

BUREAU OF LAND MANAGEMENT The nation's biggest land
agency: **www.blm.gov**

NATIONAL PARK SERVICE The NPS Web site is packed with
information on all of the national parks. Here you will find
maps, history, culture, nature, science, and more:
www.nps.gov

RECREATION.GOV Information on recreation on all federal
public lands: **www.recreation.gov**

U.S. GEOLOGICAL SURVEY A great Web site with a scientific
approach to maps, imagery, and publications: **www.usgs.gov**

U.S. FISH & WILDLIFE SERVICE Manages millions of acres of wild
national wildlife refuges and game ranges: **www.fws.gov**

U.S. FOREST SERVICE The USFS site offers info on all forest-
service land. The maps, brochures, and information on recreational activities are top-notch: **www.fs.fed.us**

FUN AND GAMES

GEOCACHING This is the official global GPS cache-hunt site. It includes pages on how to get started, how to hide and see a cache, how to find a benchmark, shop for gear, sign up for membership, purchase trackable items, participate in forums, and more: **www.geocaching.com**

LETTERBOXING This Web site covers the specifics of letter-boxing in North America. There are pages on getting started, clues, travelers, searching for boxes, regalia, kids, talk lists, and a glossary: **www.letterboxing.org**

MAP RESOURCES

These sites are my favorites, along with the maps offered by the federal and state agencies listed at left.

MAPQUEST **www.mapquest.com**

NATIONAL GEOGRAPHIC **www.nationalgeographic.com/map machine** or **www.nationalgeographic.com/maps**

TRAILS.COM **www.trails.com**

TOPO USA **www.topousa.com**

OVERALL FAVORITE INFORMATION SOURCES

AWAY.COM **www.away.com**

BACKCOUNTRY.COM National scenic-trails mailing list: **www.backcountry.com**

BACKPACKER MAGAZINE **www.backpacker.com**

BACKPACKGEAR TEST **www.backpackgeartest.org**

smart& **savvy** hiking

KIDS HEALTH **www.kidshealth.org**

OUTDOOR DIVAS **www.outdoordivas.com**

OUTDOOR GEAR SWAP **www.outdoorgearswap.com**

SLACKPACKER **www.slackpacker.com**

TREKALONG.COM **www.trekalong.com**

Index

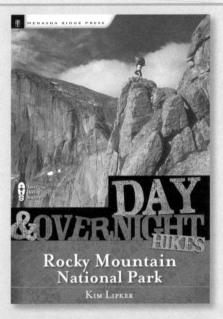

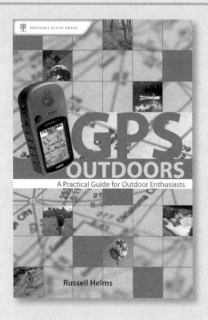

DEAR CUSTOMERS AND FRIENDS,

SUPPORTING YOUR INTEREST IN OUTDOOR ADVENTURE, travel, and an active lifestyle is central to our operations, from the authors we choose to the locations we detail to the way we design our books. Menasha Ridge Press was incorporated in 1982 by a group of veteran outdoorsmen and professional outfitters. For 25 years now, we've specialized in creating books that benefit the outdoors enthusiast.

Almost immediately, Menasha Ridge Press earned a reputation for revolutionizing outdoors- and travel-guidebook publishing. For such activities as canoeing, kayaking, hiking, backpacking, and mountain biking, we established new standards of quality that transformed the whole genre, resulting in outdoor-recreation guides of great sophistication and solid content. Menasha Ridge continues to be outdoor publishing's greatest innovator.

The folks at Menasha Ridge Press are as at home on a white-water river or mountain trail as they are editing a manuscript. The books we build for you are the best they can be, because we're responding to your needs. Plus, we use and depend on them ourselves.

We look forward to seeing you on the river or the trail. If you'd like to contact us directly, join in at www.trekalong.com or visit us at www.menasharidge.com. We thank you for your interest in our books and the natural world around us all.

SAFE TRAVELS,

Bob Sehlinger

BOB SEHLINGER
PUBLISHER